"As a loud and proud West Philadelphian, I found this volume to be a visionary and genuinely inspiring approach to chronicling the momentous events of 2020. *How We Stay Free*, with its offering of poetry, history, context and practical organizing strategies is a book that so many of us didn't even know that we needed. I am persuaded that the spirit of onetime West Philadelphia resident Paul Robeson moves through pages, which attest to Black identity as an infinite plurality and Black love as Black collective action."—**Asali Solomon**, author of *The Days of Afrekete*

"*How We Stay Free* is a foundational text and map that builds on the legacy of the Black Radical Tradition as localized in Black Philadelphia. Through this eloquent mix of poetry, prose, interviews, and archives of Philly's Black Uprising, this text places our fight for justice that year within a much longer history and future of radical revolt. This is must read for community residents, activists, organizers to model ways that Philly has paired arts-based resistance work with organized protests and mobilization to build sustainable radical coalitions for freedom." —**Dr. Christina Jackson**, scholar-activist, community facilitator, and Associate Professor of Sociology at Stockton University

"Christopher Rogers and Fajr Muhammad have curated an urgent and timely collection. *How We Stay Free* documents how the 2020 Black uprising in Philadelphia sparked the political imagination. Produced in collaboration with the Paul Robeson House and Museum, it illuminates how Paul and Eslanda Robeson remain inspiring symbols of the radical social change so urgently needed today."—**Jordan T. Camp**, author of *Incarcerating the Crisis: Freedom Struggles and the Rise of the Neoliberal State*

T0153503

"This powerful volume provides a maroon archive of Black resistance, historical memory, and survival work during the 2020 uprisings in Philadelphia. From the founding of the Philadelphia Black Radical Collective to the emergence of the Black Students Alliance in July 2020, the writings and spoken word in *How We Stay Free* remind us that, "Freedom is not a destination. It's a process."

By documenting Black Philadelphia's activist praxis during the United States' largest popular mobilization in history, this edited collection unearths the precious artifacts of local struggle through voice, material culture, poetry and prose. It connects past, present, and future by interweaving the histories of the Paul Robeson House and Museum and Hakim's Bookstore in West Philadelphia to the contemporary practices of mutual aid and survival developed by the Black and Brown Workers Cooperative to ensure that Black Trans Lives Matter.

*How We Stay Free* is a rich tapestry of political work and freedom dreams that is essential reading for understanding our city and the larger world beyond as we reckon with the COVID-19 pandemic, the scale of state violence at home and abroad, and unprecedented ecological crisis. Underneath all we do, Mike Africa, Jr.'s reminds us that "the overall mission, the grand mission itself" must be to "protect life."—**Donna Murch**, author of *Living for the City: Migration, Education, and the Rise of the Black Panther Party in Oakland, California* and *Assata Taught Me: State Violence, Racial Capitalism and the Movement for Black Lives*

"*How We Stay Free* is a living archive built by a community of freedom fighters. In its pages, readers walk the streets of West Philadelphia, stepping into Hakim's Bookstore, marching up Broad St. with the Philly Black Student Alliance, sharing food at the Bunny Hop in Malcolm X Park, or sitting in the parlor at 4951 Walnut where Paul Robeson's voice still thunders in the walls. This is poetic record of resistance from the 2020 uprisings. From the ashes of the MOVE bombing to the surviving nail where Frank Rizzo's statue once stood, these are blueprints for a future being made in the present. A beautiful compendium of struggle." —**Christina Heatherton**, coeditor of *Policing the Planet: Why the Policing Crisis Led to Black Lives Matter*

# HOW WE STAY FREE

## Notes on a Black Uprising

Edited by Christopher R. Rogers, Fajr Muhammad,
and the Paul Robeson House & Museum

ISBN: 978-1-94217-350-2 | EBook ISBN: 978-1-94217-362-5
Library of Congress Number: 2021948798

10 9 8 7 6 5 4 3 2 1

Common Notions                    Common Notions
c/o Interference Archive          c/o Making Worlds Bookstore
314 7th St.                       210 S. 45th St.
Brooklyn, NY 11215                Philadelphia, PA 19104

www.commonnotions.org
info@commonnotions.org

Discounted bulk quantities of our books are available for organizing,
educational, or fundraising purposes. Please contact Common Notions at the
address above for more information.

Cover design by Josh MacPhee / Antumbra Design
Layout design and typesetting by Morgan Buck / Antumbra Design
Antumbra Design www.antumbradesign.org

Printed by union labor in Canada on acid-free, recycled paper

# HOW WE STAY FREE

## Notes on a Black Uprising

### Edited by Christopher R. Rogers, Fajr Muhammad, and the Paul Robeson House & Museum

Brooklyn, NY
Philadelphia, PA
commonnotions.org

The editors of this anthology, in solidarity with the community of contributors that made this project possible, offer this special collective dedication:

*We honor those who have transitioned, some in 2020 but also before, from whom we have inherited the struggle.*

Conrad Africa. Consuewella Africa. Delbert Africa. Delisha Africa. Doretha Africa. Life Africa. Lil Phil Africa. Merle Africa. Netta Africa. Nick Africa. Phil Africa. Raymond Africa. Rhonda Africa. Tomaso Africa. Tree Africa. Melody Ellen Beverly. Edward Collier. Charles E. Crews. Beryl Davis. Dominique "Rem'mie" Fells. Robert Forbes. Garrett Foster. Loretta Garcia. Kelly Girl. Dawoud Hakim. Norise Harris. Louise Elizabeth Jones. Gail Wendy Lowe. James T. Lowe Sr. Adrian Erik |McCray. LJ McFarland. Saboor Muhammad. Barry Perkins. Linda Richardson. Mario Riley. James "Juju" Scurlock. Frank Lloyd Stephens. Na Tanyá Daviná Stewart. Summer Taylor. Jacqueline Tindal. Walter Wallace Jr. Geneva Young. Paul and Eslanda Robeson.

*We honor those who may be currently locked inside or standing trial, recognizing that our road to liberation is bound with their freedom.*

Mumia Abu-Jamal. Lore Elizabeth Blumenthal. David Bobo. Matthew Early. Pete Guerra. Leaf. Nichol Lee. Russell Maroon Shoatz, Sr. Ant Smith. Kwame Teague. All political prisoners, until all prisons cease to exist.

*We lift up the names and lives of our next generation, those newly entering this world, to whom we will pass the baton to continue the worthy work.*

Sumiaya Abdur-Rasheed. Fuseina Dashini Abukari. Amara. Ayah. Journee Ayers. Kamila Skye Blackburn. Brielle. Kameron Brown. Keon Brown Jr. Coltrane. Compton. Emma. Evelyn. Aiden and Adeline Frey. Jamie. Jeremiah. Luca. Mathias. Mia. Avery Miller. Dahra Mshinda. Nafis, Elijah and Zameer Muhammad. Thelonious Palacio. Prince. Gary Richardson III. Mia, Emory, and Eli Rogers. Logan Serraty. Theo. Sean. Shiloh Sage Amaris Wilson. Zakiya. To all our Black children.

**The *How We Stay Free* Project Team**

This project would not be possible without the openness, willingness, and generosity of time of our contributors, and the editors who pledged to labor with us along this journey: Maya Arthur, Jasmine Combs, and Jared Michael Lowe. A grant from the Independence Media Foundation Community Voices Fund allowed us to develop this platform for community storytelling with the assistance of the literary arts nonprofit Blue Stoop. Thank you, Emma Eisenberg, for telling us to go for it. To our publisher Common Notions, we are incredibly grateful for your support, labor, and collaborative vision in nurturing this publication into something for which we will forever be proud. We offer this sincere acknowledgement as another reminder that without community, there is no liberation.

**LEAD EDITORS**
Fajr Muhammad
Christopher R. Rogers

**EDITORIAL ASSISTANTS**
Jasmine Combs
Jared Michael Lowe
Maya Arthur

**EDITORIAL CONSULTANTS**
Emma Eisenberg
Sherry L. Howard
Vernoca L. Michael
Janice Sykes-Ross

**WEB DESIGN**
Brandi Goldsborough

# Contents

# About the West Philadelphia Cultural Alliance / Paul Robeson House & Museum

Janice Sykes-Ross, Executive Director

The West Philadelphia Cultural Alliance was founded in 1984 by librarian Frances P. Aulston to stimulate community participation in the arts by cultivating an interest in, understanding of, and appreciation for the arts in the Greater Philadelphia region. Her friend and trailblazer, Vernoca L. Michael, carried on Fran's remarkable legacy after her ancestral transition in 2015.

A year after our founding, the City of Philadelphia dropped a bomb on the MOVE headquarters in West Philadelphia that left eleven people dead. To help the city heal and restore community spirit, the Alliance—consisting of Fran and a hardy group of volunteers—assembled more than fifty organizations for a week-long arts festival. Titled "Cultural Arts Marathon – Family Time," the event included music of all types, poetry, puppet shows, and storytelling.[1]

The Alliance sought to increase its visibility and carry out its mission by buying the house at 4951 Walnut Street where Paul Leroy Robeson, Esq. lived the last ten years of his life with his sister, Marian Forsythe. Their Victorian home, built in 1911, became the Paul Robeson House & Museum, and each room chronicles a period in his life. It is a fitting legacy to a man who spoke out against injustice and oppression with his beautiful voice.

---

1. Ken Montaigne, "Cobbs Creek healing takes a cultural turn," *The Philadelphia Inquirer*, August 4, 1985, https://www.newspapers.com/image/174018348/?terms=west%20 philadelphia%20cultural%20alliance&match=1.

The Alliance's work remains as relevant today as it was thirty-seven years ago. Art as a vehicle for engaging people and effecting social change ia a hallmark of Robeson's activism.[2]

The Paul Robcson House & Museum is a place where different voices can be heard and where artists of all types are free to express themselves. Our "Arts in the Parlor" series mimics the times when Robeson sang his most famous songs in the parlor of 4951 Walnut accompanied by a pianist. Our expanded virtual programming allows us to connect with global audiences, continuing the tradition of cultivating multi-ethnic, transnational solidarity. Through our Artist in Residence program, select artists have an area inside the house to create and thrive. Our arts programs with local high schools draw students into the house to learn about Robeson's unparalleled contributions.

"As an artist I come to sing, but as a citizen, I will always speak for peace, and no one can silence me in this," Robeson said. Like our namesake, we will forever speak through the arts of our people, whether it's prose, song, dance, visual arts, or interactive media. We have fulfilled our commitment to this great man through the financial and spiritual support of all the people who recognize and acknowledge him. The people who have walked the floors he walked, climbed the stairs he climbed, and looked wondrously on his accomplishments through the photos and memorabilia at the house have sustained us.

Robeson bequeathed to us the sacred responsibility to work on the side of freedom: "To be free . . . to walk the good American earth as equal citizens, to live without fear, to enjoy the fruits of our toil, to give our children every opportunity in life—that dream which we have held so long in our hearts is today the destiny that we hold in our hands." We—and the world—will always be indebted to him.

---

2. Readers looking to learn more about the model of Paul Robeson's activism should turn to "Paul Robeson's Activist Spirit Permeates 2020 Protests" on page 7.

# Timeline of the Actions and Global Events of Summer 2020

This compilation of events provides context for the moments documented in this collection. The editors see this timeline as inexhaustible: it cannot be made to capture all the significant events and actors that contributed to the fullness of movement activity in Philadelphia during 2020. We invite readers to help us make the timeline more dynamic and complete by visiting the project online at howwestayfree.com.

## January

- (Jan 26) A legendary basketball star with Greater Philadelphia roots, Kobe Bryant, his thirteen-year-old daughter Gianna, and seven others die in a tragic helicopter crash in the hills of Calabasas, California.

- (Jan 30) The novel coronavirus (COVID-19) is declared a public health emergency of international concern. The first confirmed case of COVID-19 in North America is reported in Washington State.

## February

- (Feb 23) Ahmaud Arbery, an unarmed, twenty-five-year-old Black man, is shot to death while jogging in a neighborhood outside Brunswick, Georgia, after being pursued by two white men in a pickup truck. Neither of his pursuers, a father and son named Gregory and Travis McMichael, were arrested or charged with a crime until May 2020. Arbery's death became a national flashpoint when, two days before public outcry forced their arrest, a graphic video of the incident—filmed by a man who joined the McMicheals in pursuing Arbery—was posted online.

- (Feb 28) The first COVID-19 related death is reported in the US—though earlier deaths will come to be known and reported later—inviting increased levels of public panic, diligence, and education around the impact of the respiratory virus. US President Donald Trump emphasizes to the press that given time, the virus will "simply go away."

## March

- Grassroots, mutual-aid organizing increases scale and impact throughout Philadelphia by experimenting with tech-enabled platforms to accumulate and redistribute life-sustaining resources of direct funds, groceries, and sanitary items to communities in need.

- (Mar 13) Twenty-six-year-old Breonna Taylor is shot and killed in her home by Louisville, Kentucky police officers. The incident occurred during a botched no-knock narcotics raid, when officers forced their way into her apartment in the early morning hours. Taylor was not the target of the raid, and the suspect police were searching for was not at Taylor's home. Months later, as street-based protests reach a groundswell, Harriett's Bookshop owner Jeannine Cook and Youth Conductors travel to Louisville to distribute political-education-centered texts in support of ongoing demands for justice.

- (Mar 16) As global and national health and safety lockdowns begin, the School District of Philadelphia closes all its schools, swiftly turning toward virtual learning for all students. Universities and workplaces soon follow with work-from-home orders.

- (Mar 30) Organizers of the #No215 Jail Coalition, Decarcerate PA, Philadelphia Community Bail Fund, Philadelphia Bail Fund, and Youth Arts Self-Empowerment Project (YASP) lead a Center City protest to #FreeOurPeople and #EndCashBail, arguing that conditions in Pennsylvania's prisons and jails will exacerbate the public health crisis and leave many to die.

## April

- As global COVID-19 cases exceed one million, Dr. Ala Stanford launches the Black Doctors COVID-19 Consortium (BDCC), seeking to address the disparity in how Black Philadelphians are receiving COVID tests and arguing this specific injustice requires additional healthcare support. Dr. Stanford becomes a nationally recognized hero for her work alongside the many dedicated Black healthcare workers of the Consortium, fighting to unravel the overwhelming legacies of discrimination in healthcare for Black and low-income communities.

- (April 2) Put People First! PA organizes community members, including healthcare workers, to stage a direct action outside Hahnemann Hospital to demand the City of Philadelphia seize and reopen the hospital. Purchased by a private equity firm in 2018 and swiftly closed in 2019, journalists report that California businessman Joel Freedman was seeking rent in the amount of $1 million per month to make the facility available for public use during the COVID crisis.

## May

- (May 13) The MOVE Organization holds a rally to honor the lives lost thirty-five years ago at 62nd and Osage Street, when the City of Philadelphia dropped a bomb on its headquarters and committed to letting the fire burn. The decision resulted in eleven deaths—including five children—and leveled sixty-one homes. Councilmember Jamie Gauthier pledges to offer the city's first formal apology for the violence, yet it is without any commitment to exploring and providing reparations.

- (May 25) Forty-six-year-old Black father George Floyd is murdered by Minneapolis police. Caught on video by Black teenager Darnella Frazier, footage of the arrest shows a white police officer, Derek Chauvin, kneeling on Floyd's neck while he was pinned to the ground for more than nine minutes. During the attack, Floyd calls out "I can't breathe!" more than twenty times. As the video virally circulates around the Internet, uprisings erupt across the US, including intense action in Minneapolis when the 3rd Police Precinct building goes up in flames.

- (May 30) A reported 10,000+ protestors pour into Center City responding to numerous organizational calls for action along the

Benjamin Franklin Parkway, between the Philadelphia Museum of Art and City Hall. Public rioting, looting, and rage strike Philadelphia from the afternoon into the evening, with hotspots located in Center City, Kensington, and West Philadelphia. Based on the events, Mayor Jim Kenney calls in the National Guard to occupy targeted neighborhoods across Philadelphia.

- (May 31) As chronicled by the *The Philadelphia Inquirer*—using an assortment of eyewitness mobile videos—the Philadelphia Police Department responds to reports of looting and protests on West Philadelphia's 52nd Street with a barrage of tear gas, rubber bullets, and pepper spray. This business and residential corridor has long been a cultural and commercial center of Black Philadelphia.

## June

- (May 31–Jun 2) Philadelphia Police Department use racially targeted and excessive force to discourage protesters from exercising their constitutional and human rights. *The New York Times* features headlines about protestors pepper-sprayed without warning and those kettled with tear gas during a protest on I-676 in Center City, many of whom were later arrested.

- (Jun 2) *The Philadelphia Inquirer* prints headline "Buildings Matter, Too" for a column by architecture critic Inga Saffron, infuriating aggrieved communities and catalyzing a cadre of employees of color to address long-ignored legacies of racism, prejudice, and bias in the paper's reporting. Forty-four employees of the newspaper organize a "sick-and-tired-out" after sending an open letter to upper management.

- (Jun 3) The City of Philadelphia removes the Rizzo statue from public viewing. The oversized (nine-foot) bronze statue of Francis Lazarro "Frank" Rizzo, Sr. (1920–1991) resided on the steps of Philadelphia's Municipal Services Building—across from City Hall—from 1998 onward. Even before its installation, it was a flashpoint for Black Philadelphia organizing as Rizzo initiated and defended a climate of police abuses and championed discriminatory law-and-order policies. He served Philadelphia as policeman, Police Commissioner (1968–1971), and two-term mayor (1972–1980).

- (Jun 10) The death of twenty-seven-year-old Dominique "Rem'mie" Fells is ruled a homicide, jumpstarting an official investigation and reinvigorating local movements' calls to defend and protect Black trans lives.

- (Jun 10) Philadelphia Housing Action organizes alongside hundreds of people who are experiencing homelessness to launch encampments on the Ben Franklin Parkway, Ridge Avenue, and for squatters to take residence in empty houses across Philadelphia to demand housing. The occupation continues through October 2020 and achieves a historic, legally binding agreement with the City.

- (Jun 15) Nineteen-year-old Tallahassee-based Black Lives Matter activist Oluwatoyin Salau is found dead after being reported missing for more than a week. Salau contributed to local protests after the death of George Floyd and was also a major advocate for justice for Tony McDade, a Black transgender man shot and killed by Tallahassee police officers on May 29, 2020.

- (Jun 18) In response to widespread public calls to "Defund the Police!" and successful community petitions organized by local activist organizations, Mayor Jim Kenney cancels the proposed $19 million increase to the Philadelphia Police Department's budget.

- (Jun 23) Protestors are violently confronted by close to 100 men wielding baseball bats and hammers at the site of the Christopher Columbus statue at Marconi Plaza in South Philadelphia.

- (Jun 26) The Black Philly Radical Collective debuts its visionary "Our 13 Demands"—under the rubric "END THE WAR AGAINST BLACK PHILADELPHIANS NOW!"—at a public rally taking place at the President's House on Independence Mall. The demands, posted online, travel across and beyond the US, as a blueprint for envisioning movement goals and advancing Black liberation organizing in this moment.

## July

- (Jul 19) Black public high school students form the Philly Black Students Alliance as hub for student-led racial justice organizing across all Philadelphia schools. Combined with the Racial Justice

Organizing Committee (RJOC), they lead a march up Broad Street which centers around RJOC's "10 Demands for Radical Education Transformation."

- (Jul 23) Free Library of Philadelphia (FLP) director Siobhan Reardon resigns in response to a set of demands delivered by the newly formed Concerned Black Workers of the Free Library of Philadelphia. Their open letter, delivered in June, issued a corrective on FLP's public antiracist rhetoric, citing that no concrete steps have been taken to root out institutional racism or protect and value the lives of Black staff members.

## August

- Report is released by the City of Philadelphia indicating Black and Latinx residents have higher rates of infection, hospitalization, and death from COVID-19 than any other racial and ethnic groups.

- (Aug 23) Police officer Rusten Sheskey shoots twenty-nine-year-old Jacob Blake as he walks away from the officer toward a parked vehicle where two of his young children are sitting in Kenosha, Wisconsin. The shooting, captured by eyewitness video, leaves him partially paralyzed and in need of twenty-four-hour care. Looting and protests follow the tragic event. White Illinois teen Kyle Rittenhouse is arrested for allegedly killing two Black Lives Matter protesters and injuring a third during a Kenosha Black Lives Matter rally. In response to the persistent police violence, George Hill of the NBA's Milwaukee Bucks chooses to sit out the upcoming NBA playoff game, inciting a league-wide wildcat strike.

## September

- (Sept 29) During the first presidential debate, President Donald Trump exclaims: "Bad things happen in Philadelphia, bad things!" The comment, based on erroneous voter fraud allegations, seeks to sow doubt about the integrity of the upcoming election.

## October

- (Oct 23) Philadelphia Police shoot and kill Walter Wallace Jr., a twenty-seven-year-old Black man understood by his loved ones to be having a mental health crisis outside of his home near 61st Street and Locust Street. This egregious act reignites riots, looting, and rage throughout West Philadelphia. During the protests, Philly police are caught by activist videographers pulling a Black woman from an SUV, beating her, and separating her from her toddler-aged child. On this day, the City of Philadelphia calls for the National Guard to occupy key neighborhoods.

- (Oct 26) Educator and community activist Anthony ("Ant") Smith is arrested and taken from his home as part of a multicity sting operation led by a Trump-appointed federal prosecutor as the presidential election nears. Smith stands accused of the alleged involvement in the arson of a police vehicle during the Center City protests of May 2020. Organizing for his defense and freedom commences under the banner #FreeAntPHL.

## November

- (Nov 6) A street rally organized by local progressive community organizations gathers outside the PA Convention Center at the same time official vote counts in Philadelphia are released that push the AP and other national news outlets to call the presidential race for Joe Biden and Kamala Harris. Celebrations continue late into the Philly night.

## December

- (Dec 10) After months of local labor organizing, Philadelphia City Council unanimously passes the Black Workers Matter Economic Recovery Package—introduced by Councilmembers Helen Gym, Kenyatta Johnson, and Isaiah Thomas—ensuring over 12,000 hospitality sector workers can return to their jobs as their workplaces reopen. This coincides with ongoing 2020 organizing led by the 215 People's Alliance and Councilmember Kendra Brooks for a "Black Stimulus" that addresses support for healthcare, housing, employment, and community safety.

# Foreword

Yolanda Wisher

> *none of my ancestors knew the dates of their birth*
> —maría sabina magdalena garcía

we alter our sense of time

we altar our sense of time

we get wise before we get old

//

according to uncle baldy, great-great grandfather clarence smithfield lewis, who was virginia-born and brought his family to pennsylvania in the late 1920s, had a mysterious phrase he'd always say: "smithfield, never forget." no one knew exactly what he was committed to remembering: a stolen legacy of smoking hams, a soldier's mantra for the battlefield, a town of blacksmiths burned to the ground? what history lurked behind the much-repeated phrase of an old man, behind the name he carried like a scarab?

some of us have forgotten what we know. because it hurts, because it's too much to carry. we work with words like roots to remember, to hush a hankering for the past. we work with soil, flesh, herbs, fabric, spices, acrylic, beats, or clay to remember what was taken.

we may not always remember. but we never forget.

//

*...don't have to seek the freedom outside because the freedom its inside.*
— victoria santa cruz

every second and third friday in 1999, you could find me in october gallery on 2nd between market and arch at a series called panoramic poetry. as host, i inherited a list of three hundred black and brown poets, an army on the vanguard of creativity and revolution. multi-limbed shapeshifters of octavia's oankali sort—poets who were filmmakers, painters, lawyers, social workers, principals—real deal renaissance folks. poetry readings led me to rallies for political prisoners. buses full of poets got me to antiwar marches in dc. in the blatant light of the open mic, my mother's fights became my own.

somehow we keep remembering a freedom older than our time. we gather together to tell our truths in the fullness and brokenness of our bodies.

nellie bright-free
alain locke-free
paul robeson-free
frances ellen watkins harper-free

told we can do nothing, we try everything. run circles round these muthas. looking for a way to get free-free. freer than white, freer than rich. we make new forms and rules. make this english language our bitch.

toni cade bambara-free
mpozi tolbert-free
adrian erik mccray-free
na tanyá daviná stewart-free

all kinds of ways to be free. all kinds of blueblackprints to follow. we write and make art to never forget the mouth-feel, the soul-feel, the sleight of hand that is freedom. we take the art of our bodies to the streets to raise the hell we are handed from the earth.

we stay black and live to die on our own terms. for the freedom inside and out. we live in the wind of our ancestors still blowing through this country. we live out their every wish, wish beyond us for the children who are coming. we teach them how to breathe with fire. watch them make the freedom that hasn't arrived yet, beyond funky in its knowing.

# Introduction

Christopher R. Rogers and Fajr Muhammad

> *But to fulfill our responsibilities as Americans, we must unite, especially*
> *we Negro people. We must know our strength. We are the decisive force.*
> *That's why they terrorize us. That's why they fear us. And if we unite in all*
> *our might, this world can fast be changed. Let us create that unity now.*
>
> —Paul Robeson, address at Welcome Home Rally,
> Rockland Palace, New York City, June 19, 1949, under
> the auspices of the Council on African Affairs[1]

> *Don't say it's impossible to change this.*
>
> —Paul Robeson, "Here's My Story," in *Freedom*,
> February 1951

Freedom is not a destination. It's a process. It's a commitment. It's praxis. It's an insistence on worldmaking possibilities in every moment of crisis. Freedom requires that we must make witness of our unique differences in the effort to cultivate sustained relations toward worlds driven by care, love, and transformation. Freedom requires that we reject the seductive entrapments of the colonizer, because our radical imagination insists on creating, returning to, *otherwise*.[2] We make freedom with what we have, because like L.T.D.'s classic *Love Ballad* goes, freedom knows what we have is so much more than they can see.

---

1. Both Paul Robeson quotes are pulled from *Paul Robeson Speaks: Writings, Speeches, and Interviews, a Centennial Celebration* (New York: Citadel Press, 1978), 210, 270

2. Saidiya Hartman, *Wayward Lives, Beautiful Experiments: Intimate Histories of Riotous Black Girls, Troublesome Women, and Queer Radicals* (New York: WW Norton & Company, 2019).

James Baldwin reminded us that the path to true freedom involves staying true to our ancestral inheritance. Here we stand. "Not only was I not born to be a slave: I was not born to hope to become the equal of the slave-master."[3] Freedom need not seek permission, nor recognition, nor validation. Freedom thrives in the "Be" class, the folkloric status of High John de Conquer elaborated by Zora Neale Hurston, as to say it shall "be here when the ruthless man comes, and be here when he is gone."[4] Assuredly, the occasion to grasp freedom is ever present. Toni Cade Bambara made the challenge clear for us. "What are you going to do to be free?"[5] echoes across the maelstrom of Black life, whether in Philadelphia, Minneapolis, Louisville, Bogota, Cape Town, Port-au-Prince, and elsewhere throughout the Pan-African world. It's in our hands, feet, hearts, and souls. We win from within.[6]

This is the premise of *How We Stay Free: Notes on a Black Uprising*. In immediate response to police terror and the murders of George Floyd, Ahmaud Arbery, Breonna Taylor, and Walter Wallace Jr., we witnessed one of the largest networked global mobilizations of our generation, reinvigorating long-standing organizing under the banner of abolition and Black liberation. What we witnessed throughout the US in 2020 was an insurrectionary moment, a chaotic and improvised movement that exemplifies the power that Black communities can wield by practicing shared freedom, sovereignty, and ungovernability. To say that the strategies used over the summer of 2020—mass protest, community mobilization, coalition building, mutual aid—are unprecedented is to discredit the collective pool of Black genius that underlies the Black Radical Tradition.[7] We've been here before. We cull these notes from organizers, storytellers, artists, and archivists to recognize that the 2020 Black Uprising in Philadelphia is part of the long, multifaceted, and continuously unfolding history of intelligence gathered from struggle

3. James Baldwin, *The Price of the Ticket: Collected Nonfiction, 1948–1985* (New York: Macmillan, 1985).

4. Zora Neale Hurston, *High John de Conqueror*, in *Hurston: Folklore, Memoirs, and Other Writings*, ed. Cheryl Wall (New York: Library of America, 1995).

5. Toni Cade Bambara, *The Salt Eaters* (New York: Vintage, 1992).

6. Hurston, *High John de Conqueror*.

7. Cedric J. Robinson, *Black Marxism, Revised and Updated Third Edition: The Making of the Black Radical Tradition* (Chapel Hill: University of North Carolina Press, 2020).

meant to once and for all do away with the chains of an order that has never served us. Underneath the nationalist myths of founding liberty, Philadelphia has always been a groundswell of rebellious underground activity; particularly of Black conspiring and coalition-building towards true freedom. While the stories archived in these pages speak to the work in one city, they are meant to be understood as a contribution to this global tradition, for the generations ahead of us to study, extend, and renew the worthy work in their own communities.

Paul Robeson too, knew far too well that we, African people, stood to be more than victims, but victors. He knew that within our principled unity lies an incredible reservoir of power. "Don't say it's impossible to change this. We must know our strength. We are the decisive force." These are the words of the tallest tree in our forest, the Great Forerunner.[8] We must not forget that Eslanda Robeson, his lifelong wife, first manager, and political trailblazer in her own right, was there with Paul, a key interlocutor in developing his singular legacy. Eslanda believed "[i]n fighting a just cause, in resisting oppression, there is dignity."[9] We must know that none of our leaders stand on an island but are enriched by a community of freedom fighters whose full histories may never be recovered yet through the deeds of a named few. As you read what's documented in *How We Stay Free*, know that it can never be the full story nor does it pretend to capture the genuine contributions of all who were there.

The Robesons' legacy inspired Frances P. "Mama Fran" Aulston, the infinitely wise and unrelenting Black community librarian and arts administrator, to fundraise and to turn the last home Paul Robeson knew, 4951 Walnut Street, into the Paul Robeson House & Museum. As Mama Fran said, "We never had no money, but we never let that stop us." Making a way out of no way and setting forward the futures our ancestors envisioned has been the energy keeping the Robeson House & Museum alive all these years. It is pulsing with the rhythms of West Philadelphia and generations of Philadelphia's Black cultural workers.

---

8. See special issue of *Freedomways* entitled *Paul Robeson: The Great Forerunner*, *Freedomways* 11, no. 1 (1971).

9. Barbara Ransby, *Eslanda: The Large and Unconventional life of Mrs. Paul Robeson* (New Haven: Yale University Press, 2013).

We view the arts as a tool of social change and in documenting our resistance in these essays, poetry, and conversations we create mighty tools to carve new ways of being. Angela Davis, recalling the artistic contributions of Paul Robeson, once acknowledged: "Progressive art can assist people to learn not only about the objective forces at work in the society in which they live, but also about the intensely social character of their interior lives."[10] We hold on to this sacred responsibility of the arts, to anchor our aspirations in that which must awaken those affected by it to creatively transform their worlds. It's the path that Uncle Paul and Mama Fran laid for us.

What would be the Robesons' role in such a moment as 2020? How would they address the revolutionary possibilities floating in the wind at the same time when so many within our communities were struggling through loss and grief? The stories in this collection take many forms, reflecting the different actions and organizing practices that fueled the multilayered movement activity over the course of the year. It was important for us to not be overly focused on spectacle, but on strategy; nor on individuals alone, but rather their work with formal organizations in shaping collective consciousness. As Kiese Laymon says, "Collective freedom is impossible without interpersonal repair,"[11] so we deeply consider what healing looks like for us. The communal position of these pieces allows them to speak to one another in ways that are unconcerned with outward conversation or justification. These stories invite celebration, recommitment, and dedication to everything that sustains us.

In this collection, the Black Philly Radical Collective teaches us about the role of crafting visionary demands that may unite a broad-based radical political coalition, while anchoring its practice in the everyday work of "showing up." Jaz Riley shows us that the practice of being radical shows up in simple but profound gestures of community care. Tafari Robertson invites us into the legacy of Hakim's Bookstore, located on 52nd Street in West Philadelphia, where Ms. Yvonne and Ms. Glenda teach us the importance of immersing oneself within texts

---

10. Tschabalala Self and Angela Y. Davis, *Art on the Frontline: Mandate for a People's Culture* (Cologne: Walther König/Afterall Books, 2021).

11. Kiese Laymon, "What We Owe and Are Owed," *New York Magazine*, May 10, 2021, https://nymag.com/article/2021/05/what-we-owe-and-are-owed.html.

to cultivate a resilient and rebellious knowledge-of-self. Cassie Owens reports on the myriad strategies that Black Philadelphians have taken to mourn, grieve, cope, and nonetheless, insist upon crafting beautiful tomorrows in the wake of persistent loss.

In this assemblage there is the natural variety of form, texture, and tenor that Ashon Crawley sees as a signature of the Black radical imagination: "It seems to me, when contending with the force and verve and movement of Black life, they couldn't confine themselves to a certain form. . . . They had to be textured, layered, in their exploration and elaboration of the textures and layers of Black sociality."[12] This texture is part of Jeannine Cook's retelling of their activism throughout Kentucky in defense of Breonna Taylor. Weaving in song, quotations, and history, the founder of Harriet's Bookshop tells the generational story of leaning on and cultivating young movement leaders. Layers abound in activist Adul-Aliy Muhammad's piece on the March for Black Trans Lives and the legacy and ongoing momentum of queer activism in the city. Poets like Ewuare Osayande, Duiji Mshinda, Jasmine Combs, and Charlyn Griffith-Oro show us why verse is not a luxury for our movements, blending critical insight and sacred wisdom to remind us of the Audre Lorde maxim: "I can feel, therefore I can be free."[13]

Poems, essays, and archival work convene to form a political quilting, as Barbara Ransby has noted, "that forges strong and reinforcing ties between our various communities, organizations, and movement sectors as we work to connect all the strands, to stitch—or weave together—disparate patches of struggle."[14] Philadelphia Housing Action gives us a timeline of the historic encampment and occupation of the Benjamin Franklin Parkway that invigorated a bold, uncompromising vision of housing justice, organized by those who stood most impacted by the city's neglect. They challenge our campaigns to advance an ethics that requires intimate commitment, revolutionary patience, and compassionate presence. The Philly Black Students Alliance writes of being galvanized to organize Black students into a political force,

---

12. Ashon T. Crawley, *The Lonely Letters* (Durham: Duke University Press, 2020).

13. Audre Lorde, *Sister Outsider: Essays and Speeches* (New York: Penguin Classics, 2020).

14. Barbara Ransby, *Making All Black Lives Matter* (Oakland: University of California Press, 2018).

drawing on legacies of the Black Panther Party that had its own origins in study groups led by Black youth.

In bringing this work together, we've reflected on the necessity and utility of this form of documentation. Abolitionist organizer Mariame Kaba urges young activists to document their practice as a lodestar to guide and ground the work. "It helps people coming after you to have something to hold onto."[15] While *How We Stay Free* is far from a definitive map of the movement work in Philadelphia, it is a living archive to be held onto, read, studied, and shared. These are not the final products of movements but steps in a long process to build, revise, and reflect on your own connection and relationship with the work of liberation.

---

15. Mariame Kaba and Solana Rice, "Practicing Imagination," *The Forge*, May 17, 2021, https://forgeorganizing.org/article/practicing-imagination.

# Paul Robeson's Activist Spirit Permeates 2020 Protests

Sherry L. Howard and Vernoca L. Michael

The people's faces were as serious as their cause. The photo showed only seven of them in a single line walking earnestly in front of the Ford Theater in Baltimore. They were protesting the theater's Jim Crow segregationist policy of forcing Black people to buy full-price tickets, walk down an alley, climb three flights of stairs, and sit in the last rows of the second balcony to watch a show. Dressed in his familiar suit and hat, Paul Robeson was near the head of the line of NAACP members bucking a system that at times seemed immovable. It was a spot that he knew so well when he joined the marchers in 1948.

Baltimore was a fitting place for Robeson. Since the 1930s, activists in the city had advocated national laws to make lynching a crime and had organized against police brutality. In fact, they had marched on the state capital in 1942 after the police shooting of a Black soldier.[1] For nearly twenty years, Robeson had eschewed a comfortable existence as an actor and singer to become an agitator for Black people. After spending years of viewing acting as merely a craft, he realized that it had to be more. His immense talents—including his deep bass-baritone voice that produced so elegant a sound—had to be used universally for good. His spirit of defiance and activism should permeate any subsequent resistance movement in this country. He used the power of his voice in songs and speeches to ensure that Black Americans lived as equals.

The Black Lives Matter (BLM) protests in response to the killing of George Floyd, Breonna Taylor, and too many others in 2020 encompassed crowds as large as a city. Robeson's minimalist group of protesters in Baltimore—just as others in the North and South at the time—had no such safety in numbers (even though that did not shield some 2020 protesters), only their bravery and steadfast commitment to their cause. Like BLM today, his protestations went beyond brutality against Black people but to the right for us to live as freely as other Americans without racial limitations. If he were alive, Robeson would have been in the thick of the protests, carrying his own "I Can't Breathe" sign. He embraced collective action, enduring peace, and the oneness of mankind.

---

1. See "1930–1965: The Great Depression and World War II," https://baltimoreheritage. github.io/civil-rights-heritage/1930-1965/.

Robeson always saw America as his home. The house (as America is dubbed in one of his familiar songs) he lived in had its broken windows, scarred walls and awful neighbors, but it was also the place built on the backs of his ancestors. He felt it his duty to confront its inequities. In Robeson's day, vigilante white mobs aided by police brazenly snuffed out Black life without punishment. Robeson worked tirelessly against the crime of lynching through an organization that advocated for national antilynching legislation. He and members of the American Crusade Against Lynching, which he headed, protested in front of Truman's White House in 1946. They met with the president; he told them the time wasn't right. Robeson assured him that Blacks would protect themselves if the government would not.[2] Afterward, Robeson spoke and sang in the rain at the Lincoln Memorial.

In 1951, he was a member of a delegation that presented an antilynching petition to the United Nations. He had always been at the forefront—long before Dr. Martin Luther King Jr., Malcolm X, the Montgomery bus boycott, and the long hard road of the civil rights struggle. He paid dearly for his activism—record companies ignored him, his speaking engagements dried up, his supporters were attacked, he and his wife Eslanda's passports were denied—cutting off a main source of his income. The FBI kept a file on him until the day he died in 1976.

He spurned the House Un-American Activities Committee (HUAC) when members tried to force him to admit that he was a Communist. "I am not being tried for whether I am a Communist, I am being tried for fighting for the rights of my people, who are still second-class citizens in this United States of America," Robeson said in 1956. Both he and Eslanda refused to answer. He returned to Peekskill, NY for a second concert after a mob of white veterans, police, and others attacked supporters who had come to hear him speak and sing. This time he was more protected, but some of his followers were attacked as they drove away in cars and on buses.

Robeson's message was so affecting that he had just as many friends as enemies both in this country and abroad. With his passport voided,

---

2. See "American Crusade Against Lynching," https://en.wikipedia.org/wiki/American_Crusade_Against_Lynching.

he performed live in the first transatlantic concert from New York to London through an underwater telephone cable in 1952. He stood on a flat-bed truck at the International Peace Arch in Blaine, Washington in 1957 and sang to a crowd of Americans and Canadians on both sides of the border.

Despite the campaign to silence him, he never capitulated. in 1955, as Robeson awaited the resoration of his passport, the white men who had murdered Emmett Till in Mississippi were acquitted. Robeson sent a telegram to activist and labor leader A. Philip Randolph, president of the Brotherhood of Sleeping Car Porters (BSCP): "Outrageous acquittal of lynchers is grim warning that our people must unite as never before in militant resistance to terror and oppression. In this hour of crisis, I stand as always with my people and offer all that I have. My heart. My strength. My devotion to our common cause."[3]

---

3. Telegram from Paul Robeson to A. Philip Randolph, September 24, 1955, Library of Congress, https://www.loc.gov/exhibits/civil-rights-act/civil-rights-era.html.

# Tincture

DuiJi Mshinda

**I.**
the healing hurts
old wounds ignored
old bones broken
compound and sticky
slick with the stuff of life

never set
never rested
never given time
or a moment to process
this barrage
this torrent

this torment
of working through pain
heavy lifting across the atlas
this searching for sane
slivers among expansive insanity

we unfortunate contortionists
forced to fit beyond the margins
of invisible lines
in between the narrow confines
of white imagination
tragic this paradigm
that passes for humanity

and asks for my worth
this land of my birth
where my search
for understanding
be demanding
my compassion

my patience
my tolerance
but never my rage
I'm supposed to keep that
locked
in a fragile cage
of endurance

endure this
poverty
oppression
stigma
infection
hatred
rejection
apathy
misdirection
shallow kindness
empty gestures
broken promises
hollow lectures
bear witness
blind listless
finding isthmus

**II.**
a thin line
a fine thread
of community
woven together

by text messages
marathon phone calls
genuine zoom interactions
as we develop
novel ways
of sharing our truth
while maintaining our distance
the implicit resistance
found in reflecting
our shared divinity
this symmetry
of holding space
and forming bonds
shields us in a world
that vilifies us upon arrival

we are focused on survival
so I may be distracted
waiting
watching
these fascists
tightening the grip
on their batons
better to bash
the skulls of
litany beyond number

we lose track of
the tears we've wept
for breonna, sandra, tanisha,
george, ahmad, amadou
waking up every morning
wondering what imma do...
for rodney, martin, malcolm, emmett, fred,
if they don't beat us we just turn up dead

and white amerikkka is shocked again
and again we say "never again"
until the "fire next time" is sparked
and the "dream deferred explodes"
as the stamina of oppressed folks'
becomes fatally overdrawn

"Pandemic!"
"Pandemic!"
anthemic outcries of disparity

we don't need
any more
heroes
martyrs
or sacrificial lambs
we do need
our fellow Americans
to see with open eyes
listen without interrupting
get over yourselves
AND
tell your people to stop killing us!

while we carry the ghosts
of our trauma
within us
the police
continuously
bruise flesh
break bones
crush windpipes
and dispose of bodies
forgotten

worth less
in spite of the hard facts
that the wealth of this nation

was built on our scarred backs
and the extermination
of Indigenous people

**III.**
the audacity
of white amerikkkans
is without peer

thievery
given pretty policy names
manifest destiny
eminent domain

you have been complicit
in our suffering for quite some time
every time you made excuses
or looked the other way
as another Black body
gets carted away
DOA

and the report says
"suspect resisted arrest"
and the politicians say
"hey, they're doing their best"

"we don't believe you
you need more people"
you need more proof
to show me that we're equal

posting is cool
and protesting is great
but we're gonna need you
to "keep that same energy"

when it's time
>> to hire
>> to legislate
>> approve loans
>> approve budgets
>> educate

believe oppressed people
when we speak of atrocities
you can't imagine

Black minds splinter
into shrapnel and shards
Black spines shatter
into pebbles and rubble
Black lives matter
why does this concept
cause you so much trouble?
we been doing this work

pick up a fucking shovel.

# The Practice of Being Radical

Jaz Riley

The shades of gorgeous Brown skin that dot the unkempt streets of West Philly bring a calm that allows me to move purposefully. The long lines and too loud conversations make trips to the local grocery feel like neighborhood adventures that double as history lessons in my imagination. Lessons that started in Memphis, where I grew up; continue in Norfolk, where I worked; and survive in Los Angeles' last Black bastion, Leimert Park, where I learned to love my queerness. I am not a native of Philadelphia, but what I have experienced here feels profoundly familiar. From spontaneous yet carefully curated queer kickbacks to the collective grief inspired by the unwieldly breadth of Black death at the hands of the state, Philly represents Black social life and all of its inherent knowledge.

I was introduced to Black feminism through Philly's neo soul music of the 2000s and the spoken word poetry scene. On-the-fly debates I witnessed between women writing their way to freedom and men trying to acknowledge and unlearn their toxicity taught me about liberation long before I knew personal spats were sources of education. From these circles, processing and rehearsing my writing with others allowed for a sense of dialogue which encouraged me to speak about the events and thoughts that influenced each piece. In these seemingly banal moments where we validated our experiences, we were challenging our values and calling in our friends to do better by each other. These folks introduced me to the language of *radical*. Black women named their personal experiences to argue against any notion that Black patriarchy or capitalism will liberate us from the stronghold of white supremacy and its attendant evils. Black women taught me that to be radical, we must seek and destroy the roots of any tree that might make a home for anti-Blackness. To do otherwise is itself anti-Black. Philly offered me a host of other lessons in the summer of 2020.

That summer's protests surrounding George Floyd's murder, alongside those of countless other Black people, highlighted an intimacy between Black lives and protest where our dissent felt, and continues to feel, never-ending. The unsurprising decision of Philly officials to overwhelm Black neighborhoods with police and military presence was a clear message that our communities were under siege. The city's efforts coincided with patterns of racial capitalism, wherein the (de)value of racialized people's livelihood gets routed to commodification through enforcements of brazen terror intended to debilitate any efforts to disrupt the system.

But the people's resistance persisted because of an embodied knowledge of the fact that the state's violation of our personhood is nonstop. Black and Brown folk who inform the tenors of life on 57th Street brought protests to my front door while confronting racial capitalism's less than covert mode of devaluation. My neighbors refused to normalize the extraordinary conditions created by a pandemic—a stilted consumerism and hyper-exploitation of the lowest wage laborers—and the ordinary nature of the US' brand of oppression— co-opting pretty words and the language of the oppressed to package their manipulation. The people extended an overt invitation to the community to take what they needed from the Rite Aid on the corner or the Family Dollar across the street without regard for corporate entities. Neighbors propped open the store doors as neglected Black folk palmed laundry detergent, box fans, and food without concern for cost, police, scarcity, or criminality. People refused their roles as consumers, all while being in lockstep with the rest of West Philly, as if we strategically planned and coordinated our responses to witnessing racial capitalism's nature. We refused the intended intimidation of police and military presence in cordoned-off streets. We redirected our labor, which is typically exhausted through concern for disruptive police tactics, to actions meant to convey our deep frustration with and a visceral comprehension of the structural components of racial capitalism.

Before I could process how this different protest action was a form of resistance that had been brewing for generations, I was forced to articulate my relationship to the police more directly. My car was shot multiple times while it was parked in front of my house—it had been there for weeks because, like many others, my partner and I were home because of the pandemic. I was only made aware of the incident when we took out our trash. An onslaught of parked police cars greeted us on both sides of the street. Yellow caution tape marked the limits of criminality while a swarm of plainclothes officers moved about the neighborhood. Our block had been barricaded indicating that something bad happened there, that bad people in need of city intervention were occupying that area. Their rapidly expanding presence felt intimidating and terrifying, triggering a rehashing of every police encounter I had ever endured in one visceral motion. I was suppressing rage from being trailed for twenty miles by police on a road trip from Tennessee to California. I recoiled in fear while remembering a Mississippi sheriff's deputy speeding past cars, stopping traffic, and flagging me down. I was resisting feeling like the scared child arrested in a Memphis high school for arguing with another Black girl. In this same breath, I noticed a spry and spirited Black man sitting on my front steps in hysterics. In the less than three minutes that I had been outside on my curb, several officers approached the man as he oscillated from being slumped over to sitting upright with his hands to his face wiping his tears and covering his mouth. The police kept asking him if he saw the shooter and if he knew the shooter, only to be met with his tearful silence. It was clear to me that those were not the questions this man needed or wanted to hear.

When officers ventured to another area of the crime scene they had marked off, I carefully approached him and asked if I could do anything for him—give him a tissue, a bottle of water, or call someone. With his head down, he tearfully mumbled that he thought he had been shot, but he used the cars to shield himself. While he had little to say to the officers, he told me he just wanted to go home but his partner was not around to let him in. He was taking a moment under extreme duress to tend to what mattered: his welfare. He exhibited an embodied rejection of the state by denying legitimacy to the police's concerns and refusing their mythical status as wholesale authority figures dictating Black life's trajectory when in their presence.

It was clear to me that this man of few words and a waterfall of tears needed safety. I was not certain I could provide this, but his safety while being chided by police took precedence over anything else that was happening. I felt an instinctual jolt that I have felt before when in police presence. No matter what gender or positionality—asserted as victim or criminal—Black people near the police are always in danger. And like the protests revealed, we do not have a savior, so we create our own weapons with which to strip the terror of imperialism, capitalism, and anti-Blackness from its roots, even if it is something like vigilance. The fact is: to work a problem from its roots rather than patching holes is the radical move. This knowledge in praxis is how some people arrive at a police abolition stance.

Through sheer adrenaline, I asked the police when they approached me why they were still questioning this man about a shooter when he was so clearly distraught. They simply stated that he was a witness. I decided to stay outside and sit with him until the police left. That night, I wanted to minimize interactions with the law, care for the man, and for us both to make it out without incident. That happened.

I cannot imagine the response to overwhelming police presence upon opening my door would have been any less terrifying if I were not in Philly or the social and political moment was not filled with such an open distrust of the police. I am grateful that no bullets hit anyone that night. I was shaken by what felt like a confirmation that I would always have to consider how I can be of service to other Black people encountering the police.

Police confrontations remind us how Blackness usurps predictability. We do not know if we will survive, but hope, disdain, and (dis)interest become unquestionable kin as we become differently hypervigilant for ourselves and anyone who looks like us. While this logic-turned-action has a particular resonance with millennials and Generation Z, it is not new to my orientation towards the world.

The more recent years of my life and formal postsecondary education have helped me make sense of and carve out space in my praxis for radicalism. The summer of 2020 encouraged me to examine my relationship to radical politics, demanding that I confront and resolve any reluctance, subconscious or otherwise, around the police, upholding capitalism, and the idea that something like *Black inversion of colonialism* espoused by those newly conscious cis-het Black male poets in neosoul's heyday will liberate us. I intervene in conversations with folk who feel inclined to forward a "bad apples" argument about the police and ask folk to consider the larger structure of terror the police represent. I remind myself and others that consumerism does not equate full citizenship, and that astronomical wealth by Black people does not fracture, but reinforces, racial capitalism. Which is to say: I am acutely invested in a global obliteration of anti-Blackness and the coalition work that is necessary for this continued international praxis.

The protests and police encounters revealed that radicalism is not an identity. It is not a declaration. Rather, it is a practice, a continued unlearning, and a perpetual reimagining. My experiences in Philly have shown me that we do not happen to land in a space of radicalism. The desire to live life free of looming threats determined by race, creed, sexuality, or gender—all dynamics that inform a logic of Blackness—demands a radical disposition.

# Housing for Everyone:
# The Fight for Housing Justice

The Philadelphia Housing Action

The following is a collaborative retelling of the actions and demands of the Philadelphia Housing Action and Occupy PHA in 2020, as the city's homeless were overwhelmed by COVID-19. It is narrated by Housing Justice activists Sterling Johnson and Nadera Hood.

## Prologue

To be clear, we didn't start this War on the Homeless. It's been a war raging in Philadelphia for over forty years, with the City sweeping encampments and forcing land takeovers since the 1980s.[1] In 2020, the Office of Homeless Services (OHS) started to attack houseless residents in Center City—in collaboration with big business and tourist interests—to clear the area of the homeless for developers and tourism. The City and the Pennsylvania Convention Center started with a paltry $500,000 in an attempt to get other businesses to give to their affordable housing fund. It was miniscule compared to the $15 million subsidy the Convention Center got each year.

On February 12, 2020, a few of us met with OHS to discuss our issues and concerns. Their leadership had planned the eviction of eighty to one hundred residents without adequate and sufficient housing, who regularly slept under the protection of the Convention Center overpass and its lights. The Workers Revolutionary Collective (WRC), a self-directed cooperative of oppressed people dedicated to

---

1. Max Marin, "Inside Philly's 40-year war on homeless encampments," *Billy Penn*, February 23, 2021, https://billypenn.com/2021/02/23/philadelphia-homeless-encampment-parkway-chris-sprowal-mayor-goode-kenney/.

the end of working class-exploitation, had been doing regular outreach and had surveyed people. Their message to OHS was clear: delay the evictions until the summer and/or until the residents were provided with permanent housing. We knew that Philadelphia's shelter system would not allow for this to happen. People would have to go to a shelter first before getting any access to housing. As it stood, the system wanted to get every housing and healthcare dollar for sheltering before they would move people into proper homes.

Instead of advocating for the human rights of unhoused people, the executive management of OHS, Liz Hersh and David Holloman, were active in people's disenfranchisement. We stood before them—a room full of advocates including the Philadelphia Housing Action and Occupy PHA—detailing the harm that would occur, how moving people several blocks would create more violence, and how being pushed to more remote areas created more risk for sexual violence and overdose. But the City decided to move forward with their forced eviction of the people living under the Convention Center. In that moment, many of us were floored by their callousness but knew we had a job to do.

## March 23

We woke up before the sun and ran out of our doors to a cold, gray, rainy morning because the city had a planned eviction of houseless residents who were living under the Convention Center Passage. We hoped (but knew better) that they would postpone the eviction as it was the first day of pandemic lockdown in Philly and the US federal agency Centers for Disease Control and Prevention (CDC) recommended against breaking up encampments if private housing options were not available.

The City went forward with the eviction, which was carried out by police, Project HOME's Homeless Outreach, and OHS.[2] We watched outreach pile people into vans without providing personal protective equipment (PPE). They took a lot of the men to a shelter called Our Brothers Place, which ended up having a deadly COVID-19 outbreak weeks later. One man was assaulted by police and then medically

---

2. Anna Orso, "Philadelphia clears homeless encampment despite CDC guidance not to during coronavirus spread," *The Philadelphia Inquirer*, March 23, 2020, https://www.inquirer.com/health/coronavirus/coronavirus-covid-19-homeless-philadelphia-pennsylvania-convention-center-20200323.html.

committed instead of arrested, so we could not find him.

We left the eviction and went back to North Philly to take over our first Philadelphia Housing Authority (PHA) house. We had been inspecting vacant PHA properties and had identified a three-story, five-bedroom row home that was ready to be lived in, so we opened it up and moved some folks who had nowhere to live into it. This would be the start of a mass takeover of PHA property. We had watched our neighbors be forced out so PHA could sell viable homes they said were not viable. We would prove that they were.

## April 17

*The Inquirer* published our op-ed on the demand for empty hotels for pandemic housing.[3] However, the encampments continued to be swept.

## May 30

The Philadelphia Housing Action joined national protests and the Uprising against police violence and the murder of George Floyd. There were talks and plans to open another encampment.

## June 10

These talks and plans provided opportunity for Workers Revolutionary Collective (WRC) to initiate the Parkway encampment.[4] Situated at 22nd and Benjamin Franklin Parkway, paces from the Philadelphia Museum of Art (PMA), houseless and evicted people gathered, erecting tents and homes since the City would not provide them. A sign denoting our key demand, "Housing Now," was hung over the encampment. When WRC cofounder James Talib-Dean Campbell died, they renamed it "Camp JTD" in his honor.

---

3. Sterling Johnson and Wiley Cunningham, "The City and State Need to Do More to Help Philly's Homeless Population. What about Empty Dorms?," *The Philadelphia Inquirer*, April 23, 2020, https://www.inquirer.com/opinion/commentary/coronavirus-covid-philadelphia-homeless-housing-quarantine-20200417.html.

4. Workers Revolutionary Collective, Facebook Live video, 1:16:41, June 10, 2020, https://www.facebook.com/watch/live/?v=2957011211051462&ref=watch_permalink.

## June 26

It was a Friday afternoon. Organizers and residents walked a few blocks in the sweltering heat to meet with city officials regarding the demands of the encampment, including the transfer of vacant public property to a community land trust. PHA would not be there as they refused to come to the table.

The meeting proved to be a waste of time as city officials lied and said they had no authority over PHA and that they could not meet any of our other demands. One resident, knowing that it was all a show and waste of time, left early, showing his disgust for the farce that was on both sides. He was correct, but the rest of us remained, since playing along with their game was part of our strategy.

We walked back to the encampment angry but determined. We needed to force PHA to the table. We needed to bring the fight to their front door. We'd show them that there were consequences to their deception and if they were going to lie, then we needed to open a new front and more encampments. We needed them to see encampments opening at Love Park and closer to the Philadelphia Museum of Art, a highly visible tourist destination.

## June 28

Summer sunset over a semipermanent act of civil unrest. Tents covered the grass at Von Colln Memorial Field. The banners that hung high over 22nd and Benjamin Franklin Parkway read "Housing Now" and "Black Lives Matter." We were not camping. We were existing.

Residents with nowhere else to go made homes out of tents while thousands of vacant PHA properties lined the streets of Philly neighborhoods, some sitting with boards on the windows and doors for decades. We were simply demanding what was ours.

Earlier in the afternoon, there was a pretty bad stabbing near the encampment, and some residents, who were initially apprehensive about leaving the familiarity of Center City and making camp in North Philly, revisited the idea of moving to PHA's new $45 million headquarters. We knew PHA had a private police force, so residents packed up and we waited until 11 p.m. to start moving. Residents piled their belongings in the back of the old Ford F-150 and moved in small groups. We moved like shadows in the darkness and quickly pitched tents, hung banners, and claimed our space as we knew that we were in the midst of war. This would come to be known as "Camp Teddy."

## June 29

The early part of the day was quieter than expected. We all got to know each other and tried to iron out logistics such as porta-potties, showers, food, and how we wanted to set things up at our new home.

Around 2 p.m. one of the organizers received a cease-and-desist letter which stated that we were all criminally trespassing on PHA property and had to leave immediately. This was a wide-open lot that had been vacant and untouched for years that a lot of people came and went from at will. We would stand our ground.

Soon after the letter was received, PHA maintenance crews from the Carpenters' Union began constructing an eight-foot fence on the other side of the block. We knew that PHA would attempt to remove us. Around 7 p.m. a few members of the maintenance crews came out to install "No Trespassing" signs, demanding that we leave. We followed and ridiculed them as they did it. We told them that since we were already in the space when the signs were posted that anybody other than us would be the trespasser. You cannot put signs up after the property is being utilized. We had a group meeting and each one of us decided to stand our ground. We were prepared for a fight in the morning.

## June 30

After a night of tossing and turning and randomly waking up to thoughts or ideas about what the morning would bring, it was time to get up. Not necessarily morning but the time when everything is that eerie color that takes over the world just as darkness gives way to sunlight. We needed coffee and lots of it.

We had called for support and there were about four supporters out early in the morning. Some of the residents expressed concern over what would happen and hoped that more support would show up.

Around 7 a.m., a single PHA police car posted up to monitor, intimidate, and irritate us. By 8 a.m. there were multiple PHA police, maintenance crews, and a bulldozer on location.

We had made protest signs the night before and stood on the corner near Ridge Avenue. Residents and organizers took turns telling our stories and trying to tell the community what was happening. The police and work crews never spoke to us or asked us to leave. They just started erecting fences around us and running a bulldozer recklessly through the camp.

We put out calls for support. Community members came and stood with us. By 11 a.m. there were over one hundred of us. Media showed up. David Holloman came out for an already scheduled meeting. We sat by a tree and spoke with him as PHA fenced us in.

PHA dug holes and stuck posts in the ground that we pulled out and threw. PHA ran bulldozers towards tents and we jumped in front of them. Around 12 p.m. we were nearly fenced in with just about half of the Ridge Avenue side open. We formed a human chain that consisted of community members, encampment residents, organizers, and supporters locking arms. Shortly after we formed the human barrier, Philadelphia and PHA police came and issued orders to remove. They attempted to hand deliver a notice of criminal trespass to Jennifer Bennetch who refused to accept the letter, so they read it aloud to her.

Then without a word the bulldozer disappeared up Ridge Avenue, the maintenance crew packed up, and the police were suddenly gone. What the heck was happening? We were confused and did not know what would come next. Hours passed and the coast seemed clear. We decided to name the camp after an elderly resident named Teddy who singlehandedly blocked the bulldozer multiple times throughout the day.

We learned later, through an *Inquirer* article, that the City's Managing Director, Brian Abernathy, was being interviewed about COVID-19 when he got the call about what was happening at the PHA and he told them to stand down so as to not "fuck up" their plans to attempt to dismantle the Parkway. Abernathy resigned days later. This was big for us as the City had been saying they had no authority over PHA although the law said they did.

**July 17**

Talks stall and break off and PHA attempts evictions of the occupied houses we have seized. The City posts its first eviction notices with August 17th set the day for the encampment's closure. However, Philadelphia Housing Action/Occupy PHA continue to resist.

**August 10**

PHA holds a press event and Camp Teddy holds a counter demonstration.

**August 17**

The second eviction day arrived but this time city councilmembers stepped in and stated their intention to mediate the negotiations. We had been in contact with and welcomed them to try. Simultaneously, we were wary of city-mediated negotiation where they would be looking to declare anything a victory. With close knowledge of the system, we knew that even with more housing resources, many of them have stringent requirements like curfews, guest policies, abstinence requirements, and regular urine screenings.

This was one of the most difficult days. We spent six hours in that room going back and forth over housing issues. I was exhausted after barely sleeping, awaiting the cops to come and force us off the PHA site. We met at the Methodist church and sat in a circle with Sterling, Wiley, Irvin, Delaney, from Philadelphia Housing Action and myself, Nadera Hood of Occupy PHA, on one side. Eva, Liz, David and Larry, from Philadelphia Housing Authority, were on the other side. The primary contentions were around the benefits that we would bring back to the camps.

Our principal demand was permanent housing. So, when the City offered tiny houses or temporary vouchers or shared housing, those were all options that weren't permanent. Most people prefer to live with their immediate family in one household. They don't want to live with strangers or with people who they barely know. We knew that we could not bring back an offer that clearly was not what people wanted.

Every time the city offered a temporary option, I would bring it back to the fact that we wanted them to transfer actual houses to us. I know for myself, Nadera Hood, I wanted to have kids and a husband. That wasn't possible in one of their SROs (single room occupancies) or permanent supportive housing spaces. At the end, they refused to move on to permanent solutions. We did not agree to anything. Even with the help of the City's councilmembers, we could not get the City or the Housing Authority to admit they had the ability to give us houses. We were ready to keep going though. The previous year, Fredo and I had done a five-month Occupy PHA protest with absolutely no support. I knew we had a lot more fight in us. We weren't going to back down.

## September 1

Philadelphia Housing Action/Occupy PHA publish demands[5] and the city and PHA admit to having the power to transfer properties.

## September 9

The "final" eviction notice was issued but we continued our resistance. Roughly 600 supporters turned out to fight the eviction and barricades were expanded at Camp JTD. The City tried to send clergy to both encampments to persuade us to leave but they were shouted down and left in humiliation. Trash trucks and buses were staged on the Parkway but the police never appeared. Though we were in a heightened alert and the police would our test defenses, we did not stand down. Camp JTD even invited Mayor Jim Kenney to brunch, an invitation he declined. In this time, The U.S. Department of Housing and Urban Development, Mid-Atlantic Regional Office formally confirmed that PHA could legally transfer properties without the need for federal approval.

## September 26

At this time, the City reaches an agreement with PHA to transfer fifty vacant houses to community land trust and continues negotiation for removal of Camp JTD barricades.

## October 1

It was the afternoon, and I received a call from an unknown number. I was used to getting calls from unknown numbers, so I answered. On the other line was Larry Redican, the PHA's general counsel, and Kelvin Jeremiah, President and CEO of the PHA. Kelvin spoke in a circular manner as if unable to get his point across. It seemed he wanted a deal, but I, Nadera, could not communicate this to the City. My hunch was confirmed that we were sitting on a valuable piece of land and they needed to start construction or they would lose $50 million in tax credits. Camp Teddy was the reason they came to the table to negotiate with Camp JTD.

---

5. Philadelphia Housing Action, "Our Demands," https://philadelphiahousingaction.info/our-demands/.

I heard the deal and took the details back to the camp. The residents were ecstatic with the deal; I was lukewarm. For me, this was about the Housing Authority, but it was also personal. I wanted the PHA police disbanded immediately. I wanted Kelvin Jeremiah to be removed and humiliated for what he had done to me, my husband, my kids, and my friends. But this fight was not just about me. I knew that this is what we had come for in theory. I knew that everyone was tired and we needed a victory and to them victory meant getting off of the streets right now. Even so, I had to be honest about this offer with everyone. It would allow the camp to move into houses.

October 1 was also a little different than those nights in June, July, August, and September. It was already getting cold. The fire could only keep us so warm. I knew that I would be able to survive because I had survived much worse. I had been much colder. I had been more tired and more scared in my life. But I also had others to think about: those who had been in and out of the hospital and my family who never wavered. We had all been through a lot the past two summers. We had been staying at the camp since the last scheduled eviction, the "third and final eviction." Since then, there had been constant surveillance, with marked and unmarked cars circling the encampment. There was an ever-present helicopter filming us from above. I was afraid to leave for any amount of time.

That night, I called Sterling and Wiley to think more about this deal. Ultimately, I and the other encampment residents had made the split and it was our move that even brought the Housing Authority into the picture. I knew that any deal would be with the devil, but at the time, it was an opening to continue our battle. The week prior I had already received an email from HUD refuting every statement from their general counsel about their ability to deed us houses. We had come for their vacant houses and they were finally offering their vacant houses. We would continue dealing with the larger camp, but de-camp at Camp Teddy.

## October 26

De-camping was hard and contentious. Many people wanted to continue the fight and stay on the land. However, I had to think about the mothers that had started this all. First, they had taken the chance in

March to break the law and settle in houses. They had kept the houses and kept good relations with the neighbors. *The Inquirer* published a story at one of the houses, putting them in danger. We had to move the camp into houses quickly in other parts of Philadelphia to make it work. People would live in arrangements that some found to their liking but others were disappointed. People are allowed to have their experience and in the end we all learned a lot about what is needed to take it to the state.

There are too many complications to call this any sort of victory, but I know that we didn't start this fight. We did not transform my neighborhood into a college campus. We did not make it so that the only low-income housing required a drug screening and supervised visitation. What type of permanent housing has supervised visits? What if someone doesn't want to stop using drugs? What if the drugs are the only things keeping them sane after being bombarded with anxiety medications since they were five? What if the K2 (synthetic cannabis) and loud music soothes a person during moments of emotional distress? We are fighting for our right to have a family, to be in charge of our own lives. We didn't start this war and it definitely isn't over. We will continue to fight them on every issue.

## Epilogue

Since the encampments shut down there is still a lot going on in terms of the City of Philadelphia sweeping other encampments that are not protest encampments. We've been trying to defend and draw media attention to them since the City is barricading these new encampments every other month. We've been going back and forth with OHS and working on getting things up and running for the actual land trust. We're finally at a place where PHA is ready to start transferring the homes but not so much with the City. There's still a lot of fight left. There's a lot going on with the police and PHA, trying to start a continuing education collaborative where social workers who report to the cops will be stationed at the houses. But the people from the camps that we put into squats are still there and now we know which people are eligible to stay in the land trust. We can start working now, making things better and still working so the City does not sweep every homeless person from everywhere in the city.

After this year, I feel that we will take action the same way. It's the thing that we do. However, what's changed is we are no longer too trusting of everyone who seems to be on the same page as we are. That was something that blew up in our faces over the course of the last year. Occupy PHA was always just our small, more hood movement rather than an activist movement. I didn't know there were people there for other reasons: to make money, capitalize, wash away their guilt.

We want the community to know that you can stand up and fight for yourself even if you don't have a formal education. You don't have to have a degree or even a big movement of people behind you. Even though the camps were a really big thing, a lot of the work we did for a few years leading up to this was just us. If you get tired of something and stand up, you can get things to change. Regardless of identity, you have to treat the people around you well. In the process of this, people came up to us offering unsolicited advice and criticism. It should be known that the people that are taking action are just regular people. If you want to build the thing, go do that. Recognize that everyone out at the 2020 protests is just a regular person.

I don't know if what happened is a win but it is a big step in the right direction. We were able to house previously unhoused folks and get the City to do it. Hopefully it sets a precedent. Honestly, I don't even know what winning is. I just want us to be good to each other and hopefully we're taking care of each other. That means all of us—not just your clique. Making sure everyone has housing. It's not a matter of win or lose. It means taking care of each other, even the people you hate, and fighting for their wins too.

# Feeding Our Neighbors and Ourselves: The Mutual Aid Work of Bunny Hop

J.A. Harris

On April 4, 2020, Katie Briggs and I started the West Philadelphia Bunny Hop in Malcolm X and Cedar Park. The uptick in positive COVID-19 cases, the increase in mitigation protocols and uncertainty that we were witnessing within our neighborhoods led us to plan our first free food distribution pop-up. Initially, the plan was to set up on Saturdays, leaving it open and vague enough in case we needed to change the plan or alternate weekends.

We got produce from Philly Food Works and SHARE, and we distributed soup and snacks that were prepared from home. In the following weeks, various chef friends contributed by preparing meals for our neighbors and in our first month we were serving close to one hundred families and individuals from our tables in the park. We offered everything from food to cleaning supplies and discovered that we were able to channel our nervous energy into something that not only sustained us but supported our community.

The work of Bunny Hop began well before the summer of 2020. I began the year mourning the loss of my mother while also shifting away from a business that was no longer serving me. I had put a lot of time and energy into the 1149 Cooperative, a shared kitchen and event space in South Philadelphia, of which I was the co-owner. I spent 2019 just trying to keep the doors open with our small staff, and during our hours of operation we served lunch, rented kitchen space to various chefs, hosted events and parties, and prepped and finished meals for off-site catering. It was in this space that we catered radical events that centered Black, Brown, and Indigenous experiences and worked with all types of community-centered organizations. After two seasons of The Free Breakfast program, and as I planned a winter service, I received news that my mother was in the hospital. A little less than two weeks after she went into the hospital, my mother transitioned from this earthly plane. I had spent so much time working at 1149 and once she was gone, I was left wishing I had gotten more time with her. As I spent the rest of the year prioritizing time with my family in mourning, the 1149 Cooperative closed down.

All of that grief put a knot in my spirit. The loss pushed any fond memories to the background and the joy and purpose I found in cooking for others had waned. I know now that I had to let go of how I was doing things in order to be available for the opportunity that would become Bunny Hop. All of the connections I had built at 1149 would be the base of support that we would need.

Katie and I first met briefly at the Church of the Advocate during a People's Supper event in fall of 2018. We met again while I was hosting an open house for 1149 Cooperative, and Katie and I would continually find ways to collaborate and support one another's work, whether it be off-site catering or hosting pop-up events in the space. It was also during this time that I met and was immediately activated by Charlyn Griffith-Oro, who was then also expanding their work, the Free Brunch Program, while I was preparing to launch Free Breakfast at 1149 Cooperative. Charlyn called me a "goddess of food," and a week later we were sharing, dreaming, and planning ways to feed people together. Charlyn and Katie have been solid and constant collaborators. Whenever I look back at where the answers came from at various times in 2020, I felt like I was calling on lessons I learned working alongside either of them. This background is important because when we started Bunny Hop is not necessarily when we began.

Our ninth week of food distribution was when the world felt like it cracked wide open. In answering our communities' needs due to COVID-19, it was the first week since we began that coronavirus wasn't the lead headline. George Floyd's murder dominated the news cycle and the feelings of fear and anger that overwhelmed me at times also rooted me in my work. It wasn't the first time I thought about my life or the lives of Black people being ended by a bullet or at the hands of some police officer who was "having a hard day." But, it was the first time I felt emboldened to push back and further integrate what I have come to know about working across communities with my experience of working in grocery stores and hospitality for over two decades.

During the summer 2020 Uprising, Bunny Hop made a point to hire a facilitator, Adonis Okonkwo, to run small workshops that provided our mostly white and non-Black volunteers with language and history of critical race theory, food justice, and mutual aid. We worked directly with Urban Tree Connection, Mill Creek Urban Farm, Lancaster Farm Fresh Cooperative, and Common Market to serve more neighbors. We connected with the residents of Morris Home, Camp JTD, and Camp Teddy, and worked to provide meals and share our excess.[1] At the peak of our summer of service we provided produce and meals to as many as 1,000 people in one week. The collaborations that came as a result of people participating in mutual aid allowed me to expand on a vision of possibility and liberation.

The 2020 Black Uprising in Philadelphia reinforced the mutual aid work of Bunny Hop and shifted us from organizing small neighborhood food distributions to redistributing resources across the city. We expanded our network as we collected donations to send into Center City for protests, and volunteer interest also rose at this time. The momentum with which this all happened was not anything we could have predicted and the support from neighbors, friends, and family was nothing I had ever experienced.

Less than a week after George Floyd's murder, our immediate neighbors and volunteers living near Malcolm X Park saw police indiscriminately assault children and residents with pepper spray and tear gas. A little over a week later, we mourned the death of Dominique

---

1. Morris Home is the first residential recovery program in the country to offer comprehensive services specifically for trans- and gender non-conforming individuals. Morris Home has been a steady home for BIPOC trans- and GNC people and a fearless place of love in Philly. Camp JTD and Camp Teddy were the beloved names of the two housing justice protest encampments organized with houseless Philadelphians and Philadelphia Housing Action (PHA). For more information on this organization, please see "Housing for Everyone: The Fight for Housing Justice" in this volume.

"Rem'mie" Fells.[2] I was constantly being reminded that this pandemic—the killing of Black people by the state—never takes a break. I had grown accustomed to pressing on, even when my heart was heavy with feelings of grief.

I've learned, throughout this past year, that grief doesn't work like that, and I learned to set boundaries for myself so that I could rest, reflect, and begin to heal. It's so important to prioritize collective care and to facilitate spaces for rest, healing, and joy. I saw a great example of this in July 2020 when we gathered to celebrate the life of Rem'mie with her family and friends on 50th Street in West Philly. We cried, laughed, sang, and danced together while we laid flowers and offerings at an altar for her to keep her memory alive.

At that time, the City had been also enforcing curfews that were meant to suppress us from going out in the streets to demonstrate against the continued state violence in our neighborhoods. This restriction of people's movement throughout the city meant that individuals and families had less time in their day to work, to run errands, to take care of themselves and their loved ones in the middle of the pandemic.

We received donations of goods during the week at Malcolm X Park. People who couldn't donate supplies sent funds, and those funds went towards goods for distribution, supply purchases for prepared foods, and directly to people/organizers who asked for assistance. We asked neighbors to host smaller distributions on their porches and stoops so that we could share with neighbors who were not able to just walk up to our regular distribution spots. We were able to fully participate in an economy that existed outside of our typical experience.

As the summer drew to a close, those of us volunteering with Bunny Hop had to anticipate how our work would need to shift with the season. We embraced a theme of going inward and switched most of our distributions to delivery so that we wouldn't have to fight the elements or have volunteers out in the cold serving neighbors. We

---

2. Dominique Fells was a transgender woman murdered on June 8, 2020 in Philadelphia, allegedly by her former romantic partner, a cis Black male. "Rem'mie," as her family and friends called her, was a beloved member of her community and her death garnered national attention for the epidemic of transgender people being murdered. For more on her life and the fight for Black trans lives, please see the essay by Abdul-Aliy Muhammad in this volume.

started an indoor distribution at the Institute of Contemporary Art in October and continued to hold walk-up distribution at Franny Lou's Porch in East Kensington. Our teams got smaller as spikes in COVID-19 cases occurred across the city. We took the cue from nature, embracing reflection and rest for the colder seasons. I learned that we didn't need increasing numbers to have growth and that our impact is best measured by our ability to sustain our relationships within our volunteer core group and with our neighbors.

We had a lot of momentum when we first started doing our distributions and it was always my hope that people in different neighborhoods and blocks would find ways to share resources apart from Bunny Hop. There's a long history of organizing and mutual-aid work in Philadelphia and I see myself as a part of that history rather than set apart from it.[3] Black people, Indigenous families, folk whose culture exists outside or alongside an American identity wouldn't necessarily identify these practices as mutual aid. As I move into a full year of Bunny Hop, my wish is that we are all learning how to expand our understanding of ourselves and our neighbors so that we can continue to integrate these practices into our relationships, workplaces, and the broader community.

At the core of this work is connection and consistency. Anyone who is interested in starting and sustaining a mutual aid initiative should lean on their existing relationships, experience, and interests as the starting point. It's also important to commit to a regular schedule—be it daily, weekly, monthly, or annually. I learned a lot by committing to showing up every Saturday, rain or shine, to serve people at Cedar Park when Bunny Hop first began. I quickly learned that I was relying on the neighbors showing up as much as they were relying on me to show up to serve. I was lucky to have Katie as a cofounder of Bunny Hop, they were like a workout partner helping to motivate me. We supported each other's ideas and efforts and as Bunny Hop grew, our efforts attracted

---

3. An avenue for continued research, mutual aid organizing in Philadelphia ranges from contemporary examples such as the long-running Food Not Bombs collective, all the way back to the 1787 founding of the Free African Society by Richard Allen and Absalom Jones. Among the first organizations of its kind in the US, the Free African Society's main goal was to provide aid to newly freed Blacks so that they could gather strength and develop leaders in the community.

others who were able to support the work and vision in other ways. All of the Bunnies bring something to the equation, each of us holding to a schedule that has helped us develop a regular practice to mutually benefit those of us serving and those being served.

When people ask me how to get started, I urge them to talk to their neighbors first. If you don't know your neighbors, make a point to introduce yourself, share with the people on your block in a regular way that doesn't put you out. I know that we will never close the gaps of food access disparities all on our own and that whether we serve one person or one hundred people it is still an undertaking. It's important to make time to check in with those people you are working with and to understand what one another's expectations are and to make that a continual practice.

When we were still meeting in larger groups outdoors, we held check-ins before we shared updates. When we ran distributions, we asked neighbors what they needed or wanted, and we served them with respect. We organized ourselves into smaller teams to handle all of the various tasks from purchasing supplies, organizing drivers and volunteers, writing grants, and leading distribution sites. Throughout all of it, our ability to communicate has been the muscle that we exercise the most. Understanding the limits and bounds of my energy as well as taking breaks to reflect and rest was extremely helpful throughout this past year. With summer behind us and work still to be done, I'm looking forward to what we can continue to build together in the years to come.

# Black Trans Lives Matter

Abdul-Aliy A. Muhammad

I never could have imagined the ways my life would be shaped by my queer identity. As a Black Muslim, it took many years for me to be comfortable in the skin I'm in. Black transgender women embraced me early on and provided me with the community and safer space I needed while I was tender with my flourishing fullness. I owe my organizing work to the legacies of trans movement leaders before me and I honor them by continuing the good fight.

Last year, amidst the uprisings against state-sanctioned murder, Dominique "Rem'mie" Fells was found murdered and dismembered on June 8, 2020. This happened months after the police shot and killed Breonna Taylor and fourteen days after police officer Derek Chauvin compressed the neck of George Floyd, killing him. This is after the police murder of Tony McDade, a Black transmasculine person, killed in Tallahassee. Rem'mie's murder wasn't at the hands of the state directly, however patriarchy is intertwined with state violence and therefore connected to the intimate partner violence that ultimately stole her away from her loved ones. She was twenty-seven-years old when her life was cut short, horrifically, leaving her mother Terri Edmonds and her sisters, Desiree and Dior, to grieve for her.

Rem'mie was a bright spot and a fiery presence who let you know how she felt. While I didn't get to know her when she lived, we've been in deep conversation in her afterlife and supporting her mother as she navigates grief, interactions with the press, and prepares for the trial of her child's accused murderer. I am honored to share space with Rem'mie's family and support them through this. Dominique and so many other Black and Brown transgender women in Philadelphia, and globally, deserve the same fiery rage that compelled us to rise up in 2020.

In my organizing work over the years, I have been deeply interested in the ways our community is held together but also the ways our work sometimes represents a "house divided." It's always been true that the most marginalized people within our communities push for all of our futures, brick by brick, knocking down the infrastructures of an oppressive system. Take for example, the work of Miss Major Griffin-Gracy: a prolific organizer, a radical Black transgender woman, and iconic figure of the transgender community. Miss Major was born on October 25, 1940, a day before my birthday and forty-three years before my arrival into the world. A former sex worker, she has been a continued presence in my contemplation, as her roots are also in organizing. Miss Major and others were among the collective that changed the world for LGBTQ people with the Stonewall riots in 1969. She was also mentored by Frank "Big Black" Smith, a leader of the Attica riots in 1971.

There is Kuwasi Balagoon, a comrade, part of the Black Liberation Army, who was bisexual and died of AIDS complications while incarcerated on December 13, 1986 at the age of thirty-nine. I am forever indebted to Kuwasi for his political instructions, visions, and analyses, collected in his essays. As a Black person who lives with HIV, it reminds me that my power isn't diminished by living with chronic illness. It makes my politics and work more grounded. My work will forever be impacted by the instructions from the light gleaned from the extraordinary work of living elders and ancestors like Miss Major and Kuwasi Balagoon.

This has come to include organizing work with the Black and Brown Workers' Cooperative (BBWC). It was the depth of passion and vision of Inahs Akilah that held that formation together. On June 1, 2016, our call to action was released, framing the work that would unfold over the subsequent years. Our mission was to uproot anti-Blackness and transphobia from nonprofits in Philadelphia, to imagine collectivity outside of 501(c)3 spaces, and push for us to own our labor. The work led to the firing of Nellie Fitzpatrick, the former director of the office of LGBT Affairs for the City of Philadelphia.[1]

In Philadelphia's Gayborhood, we protested the racialized dress codes of gay bars and the practice of asking for multiple forms of ID that impacted our undocumented community. After an action outside of Icandy and other bars, a video leaked of former Icandy boss, Darryl DePiano, yelling the N-word repeatedly. This led to public outrage. While Black and Brown LGBTQ people had been expressing the impacts of surveillance and other racist encounters, non-Black people wanted "receipts" to prove that anti-Blackness existed. The video of the bar owner was released on YouTube on September 27, 2016.[2]

The movement to address racism in LGBTQ spaces grew and the Philadelphia Commission on Human Relations (PCHR) held an historic hearing on October 25, 2016. Following this, recommendations were made, and the report named the work of radical Black and Brown organizers as being instrumental in pushing the City to take action. While we were ostracized within the LGBTQ community, we continued pushing for Black liberation because the only way we all get free is by backing the movement for Black futures. In the months that followed, we started putting pressure on nonprofits named in PCHR's report, such as Philadelphia FIGHT and Mazzoni Center, which are both prominent HIV care providers in Philadelphia. Mazzoni Center lauds itself as the largest provider of LGBTQ healthcare in the region. Our organizing culminated in the resignations of the Center's medical director, its CEO, and board members. Later, the frontline workers unionized and continued putting pressure on the organization's leadership to actually live the values it claims on paper.

The BBWC understands that our work must address the displacement of Black and Brown people caused by gentrification. We have put pressure on businesses and organizations that benefit from the forced

---

1. Nellie Fitzpatrick was ousted as Director of Office of LGBT Affairs in February 2017 after immense organizing efforts to disrupt a culture of white supremacy, exclusivity, and workplace violence in the city's Gayborhood. Organizers from the Black and Brown Workers Co-op demanded her resignation after she dismissed our call for the office to have an intersectional approach when addressing community concerns.

2. See "ICandy Philadelphia Owner Uses the N-Word," https://www.youtube.com/watch?v=A3hOVbKGpfs.

removal of Black people, such as food cooperatives, fancy ice cream purveyors, and coffee shops. Our campaign #DisappearingBlackness, to counter disappearing Blackness as displacement politics, began in early 2018. We talked about how developers were usurping "councilmember prerogative," the power that district councilmembers have to decide on the use of public land within their district's borders. This campaign heavily influenced the conversation about housing and displacement during the 2019 Philadelphia City Council elections.

A cooperative led by Black and Brown LGBTQ people, with little funding, elevated the collective consciousness of our city and pushed against its long-standing racism, displacement, and nonprofits that were anti-Black, and for this we deserve our flowers. Not to rest on our laurels, but to feel the appreciation and affirmation that makes us continue our work.

In last summer's Uprising, we witnessed a collective outcry of rage spread across the US and globally. Direct actions bring a clarity of focus and provide a unified message, loudly aimed at the institutions that want us dead or worked to death. As a queer Black Muslim from Philly, I want our rage felt when our family, our friends, and our house mothers are murdered. I want us to exclaim that enough is enough!

All Black people are magical and profoundly rooted in our traditions. Across spectrums of gender identity, gender expression, sexuality, and gender performance, we are all deeply intertwined. Yet, when Black transgender women are murdered, there is a void between movement and community space. Often the work of remembrance falls on few of us to uplift the legacies of those stolen away. I challenge this: if you truly believe that freedom is the birthright of Black people and that Black lives matter, then the streets must know the names of Dominique Rem'mie Fells, Stacey Blahnik, Anthony (Alphy) McCullough (who was murdered defending a Black trans woman), Gucci Movato, Nizah Morris, Kyra Cordova, London Chanel, and so many more lost to state violence, intimate partner violence, and other forms of violence. As I've written previously:

> We must not only #SayHerName, recognizing the Black women
> we've lost—but we must dismantle the patriarchal system that
> engenders intimate partner and other violence which claims so

many of our sisters. We have to rage for Black transgender women because if we aren't shaking the grounds on which they've died, we cannot fully believe in Black lives. If we don't march for their lives, we are sidestepping their humanity. If we don't uplift Black transgender women when they are alive, we have contributed to a culture that makes their violent deaths possible.[3]

Black Trans Lives Matter.

3. Abdul-Aliy Muhammad, "As Philadelphia Mourns Dominique 'Rem'mie' Fells, Black Trans Lives Still Matter | Opinion," *The Philadelphia Inquirer*, June 25, 2020, https://www.inquirer.com/opinion/commentary/dominique-remmie-fells-philadelphia-black-trans-lives-matter-20200625.html.

# Rest for Oluwatoyin Salau[1]

Christian Hayden

Worlds whirling in
resonance with
imagining eyes
behold a scene
instead of cry
I dream

June Jordan scriptures
scribbled into sidewalks
chalks talk Black beauty emanating.
Trees bow, brothers nod to show respect,
heart and place not separate
both open for our
sacred wonderer
who's blessed us with her pondering.
Children look here yonder,
see seeds wild outstretching
essence place untamed enmeshing, echoes
each one of us contain of a note of the other,
grand symphony you can't exist without me
living liberation, queer visions see the path,
Toni smiling, say we finally found free.

---

1. Nineteen-year-old activist Oluwatoyin ("Toyin") Salau was a prominent voice in protests
   in Tallahassee after the death of George Floyd. Toyin was also a major advocate calling
   for justice for Tony McDade, a black transgender man who was shot and killed by
   Tallahassee police officers on May 29, 2020. An initial missing person report was filed
   on June 6, just hours after Toyin tweeted in detail about a man who sexually assaulted
   her after disguising himself as "a man of God," who she thought was trying to be of help.
   Her death was reported on June 15, 2020, jumpstarting a national conversation on
   valuing and protecting Black women within our movements.

Instead of cry
I breathe,
speak a world into birth,
emerging out of another,
doula midwifing
new realities, and structures
forming we
a phalanx of prophets
choosing not to speak yet
crowning the head of
a revolutionary.
Our wonderer with newfound power
a disinherited dabbling
with destroying
master's matrix
limning new language
painting safe havens
in arts and spaces
that feed Black women
so when they need to rest
it isn't only in death
but love-crested nests
that are meant to hold,
recharge, and soothe
our best

Toyin, rest.


Something struck me when I heard about Oluwatoyin ("Toyin") Salau's death, after months of death and more death. It felt like the tipping point for me. So many times Black women lead and sacrifice in public, to meet suffering and violence in private, at the hands of men who look like me. This public loss felt strangely private and familiar. I felt the times I/we failed Black women come to a crushing head. To be so seen yet invisible felt like a contradiction too cruel, something distinctly disrespectful to Toyin. Maybe numbed from the overwhelming collective suffering, I couldn't cry, but I felt I owed something to her and to Black women in general. My debt/call/responsibility was to imagine a different, freer world and work toward it. —Christian Hayden

# End the War on Black Philadelphia Now!: Crafting Demands with the Black Philly Radical Collective

Krystal Strong, YahNé Ndgo, Gabriel Bryant, and Flare of the Black Philly Radical Collective

On the morning of March 28, 2021, *How We Stay Free* coeditors Fajr Muhammad and Christopher R. Rogers sat down virtually with Krystal Strong, YahNé Ndgo, Gabriel Bryant and Flare, members of the Black Philly Radical Collective (BPRC), to discuss a wide range of topics emerging from the development and mobilization of the collective's thirteen demands.

The Black Philly Radical Collective is "a new formation of long-standing, Black-led, abolition-based organizations that have united in the fight against police terror and state violence." Signatories of the collective include: Philly for Real Justice, the Black Alliance for Peace, Black And Brown Workers Cooperative[1], Abolitionist Law Center Philadelphia[2], Abolitionist Law Center Pittsburgh, Human Rights Coalition Philadelphia, Human Rights Coalition Pittsburgh, Mike Africa Jr. of MOVE, Mobilization for Mumia, International Family and Friends of Mumia Abu Jamal, and Malcolm X Grassroots Movement.

Its treatise is a visionary abolitionist platform, delivered on June 4, 2020 under the banner "We Want Freedom: End the War Against Black Philadelphians NOW!"[3] This present text offers a focused, concise excerpt from the interview, edited for clarity.

---

1. Philadelphia-based, the BBWC defines themselves as a labor-organizing cooperative fighting contemporary forms of subjugation/dehumanization in our workplaces, classrooms, and communities by expanding democracy and agency. Learn more at https://www.blackandbrownworkerscoop.org/.

2. The Abolitionist Law Center is a public interest law firm inspired by the struggle of political and politicized prisoners and organized for the purpose of abolishing class- and race-based mass incarceration in the United States. Learn more at https://abolitionistlawcenter.org/,

3. The full "End The War on Black Philadelphia Now!" platform is included in the Appendix for reference and study on p. 149.

**Walk us through the timeline of shaping the platform "End the War on Black Philadelphia Now" for the City? When did it become apparent that a platform for demands were necessary? What meetings happened? What consensus was taken?**

**YahNé Ndgo:** We collectively decided that with everything going on [protests, looting, the National Guard occupation] we needed to leverage the reality of this moment. In the May and early June 2020 actions, we noted that while a lot of people wanted to get involved, there was a lack of clear leadership. We recognized the impact these factors were having on different mobilizations and decided there had to be movement within the Black organizing community to assume leadership in a way that was not hierarchical.

We have always recognized that the [BLM Philly chapter] operates in this Philadelphia landscape with all of this rich organizing wisdom and knowledge. Without any entity saying we alone have ALL of that wisdom and knowledge, we wanted to tap into the collective wisdom in order to create a document that would both cast a vision for what relief from this system would require and establish a plan and a movement for how to get there.

We talked about what our focus should be, for example, should we be focusing on the city level or the state level? We talked about if we should be focusing on the things that are specifically related to and relevant to police violence and police murder; to acknowledge the way this violence interacts with our communities, the myriad ways it manifests through different carceral states and carceral systems. Or did we want to expand beyond that to other things? We made the decision to focus our demands around carceral violence and issues within carceral systems. We made decisions declaring our mutual agreement that this is an abolitionist set of demands. There were pieces that didn't reference direct carceral abolition but *collectively* they do. The demands all feed this larger vision around abolition.

We spent many nights working on this collective document on Zoom. The primary writers of the demands were Krystal, Megan Malachi, and myself. Saleem Holbrook from the Abolitionist Law Center (ALC) also contributed. We got some insights from the Black and Brown Workers Cooperative (BBWC) through Dom [Dominique London]. We just continued to nurture them, refine them, and put together this language that was being shared collectively. It was happening fast, because we wanted to get them out quickly. There were more people we wanted to include. We were trying to find that balance between getting the word out to people so that they could be involved in the process and moving the process forward.

Around the same time we were bringing the demands together, there were legislators who collectively put together their own set of demands, and we had to let them know about ours, because they were prepared to be praised for something that was not praiseworthy. Theirs was a "let's get more tasers, body cams, and training" kind of approach. They didn't understand or acknowledge that people are burning down police stations because we don't need more police. We're ready for the end of these police, the walls and bars that they put our people behind, all of the systems that they use to put a thumb on our communities. We rejected their demands, and we presented our own demands.

We reorganized our list of demands and put together a website to present them to a wider public so there wasn't a singular focus on these legislator-driven reformist demands. As part of this push to promote our demands, we scheduled a press conference for June 26, 2020, at the Slavery Memorial, that served to officially debut them to the world.[4]

**Krystal Strong:** I just want to emphasize a few things. I think the immediate fallout of the May 30–31 weekend was super-important for catalyzing the idea that we need demands.[5] We need a clear set of things that we are demanding of the system and also struggling around. We also need to have a clearer understanding of the benefits in forming new kinds of relationships with each other. May 30 was one of the longest

---

4. The Slavery Memorial, formally known as the President's House, is located at 6th and Market Street in Philadelphia. It represents the spot where George Washington and his presidential successor, John Adams, lived when Philadelphia was the nation's capital during the last decade of the eighteenth century. Black-led community organizing by the Avenging the Ancestors Coalition amongst others in the mid-2000s pushed the project to emphasize the histories and contributions of enslaved Africans and Native Americans who were violently implicated in the founding of the US.

5. Ed note: on May 30, actions began on the steps of the Philadelphia Museum of Art and moved into Center City. Protestors were kettled by police and demonstrations ignited with attempts to bring the Rizzo statue down, the overturning of cars, and a police vehicle being set on fire.

days ever. It went from action, to action, to march, to kettling; and to confrontations with the police, to City Hall, to cop cars on fire, to the [Frank] Rizzo statue on fire, to that Starbucks getting lit up.[6] Modell's got bum-rushed and community members got a whole new summer wardrobe. To 52nd Street. A LOT is happening. So much is happening. What is also happening as a result is that the state is scared. The state realizes they are vulnerable. The agents of the state—the mayor, city council, the governor, the people who are the bearers of power in the system—they're nervous as hell that open rebellion will continue and a new autonomy will come into being. We know that.

It's one of the reasons why now all of a sudden everybody wants to announce things like "Oh, Rizzo!" which is the most reactionary thing, like, "OK, we'll take the Rizzo statue down." That happens within a couple of days. The state is clearly vulnerable. This is an opportunity for us to push forward on things that we've been struggling around for years, but then again, there are also people in the streets who are presenting themselves as the leaders or positioning themselves to be intermediaries to the state. These are folks who don't appear to be connected to organizations or to radical organizing work. We had a debrief right after the events of Saturday, May 30, 2020 and I cannot forget the events of Sunday. Members of the BPRC were out on 52nd Street.[7] We were tear gassed. We witnessed firsthand what happened. We saw this unbelievable mobilization—never in my life as a Philadelphian have I experienced that volume of people coming together in that way—and simultaneously, we saw some serious repression by police being mobilized.

In our debrief session, we started to assess the situation and assess the gap in coordinated organization that was showing itself at that moment. Some of the things that started to happen was state actors started to reach out to organizations to get their ears, to get them on a call with the governor, to get them on a call with the mayor. One of the things that became very clear to us is that we don't want any organization to go into that room by themselves, especially if we are

---

6. See introductory book timeline entry for June 3 for more background info on Frank Rizzo statue, xiv.

7. Ed note: See https://whyy.org/articles/the-tear-gassing-of-west-philly-a-history-told-in-police-dispatches/ for a rundown of events taking place on 52nd St on May 31, 2020.

already beginning to coordinate together. We don't want to go into those spaces by ourselves and we also don't want to go into those spaces without a plan.

What I remember from some of those early calls in the week following the events of May 30–31 is us talking seriously about: what is possible? What are our radical demands? Most of our organizations' work is not state-focused. We are not focused on asking the state for anything. Most of us are focused on building power within our communities. However, in such a moment when the state is vulnerable, we wanted to think strategically about what it would mean to make demands of the state. I remember all of us collectively, before some of us broke off to develop the ideas a bit more fully, talking about what are the opportunities.

One of the campaigns already being worked on [by some of the groups of the BPRC] was disrupting a proposed budget increase for the Philadelphia police. That seemed like a really obvious thing to struggle around. At the same time, organizations like MOVE and Philly For REAL Justice[8] were struggling around the Rizzo statue. That was an easy target. We were thinking about short-term but also long-term goals. Megan, YahNé, and myself spent a few late, late nights taking the ideas that came out of our collective sessions and trying to expand them into demand-oriented language showing a clear line about what our vision for transformation and abolition is.

**What advice and/or resources would you put forward to other Black collectives and formations who are coming together to frame demands with and on behalf of their communities?**

**Gabriel Bryant:** The work is always going to be in taking action. Oftentimes people look to collectives like ours for the street action, for the street work, and I really want to emphasize what Krystal said about building power in the neighborhoods. There were several neighborhoods

---

8. The Philadelphia Coalition for Racial Economic and Legal Justice (REAL) defines themselves as an inclusive grassroots organization that is community focused and globally engaged. Their mission is to provide a safe space for community organizations and individuals to come together and combine resources to eliminate the system of white supremacy and police terror across all areas of racial, economic, and legal oppression. Visit their archive at http://phillyrealjustice.com/.

this summer and fall [2020] that we were in repeatedly. Speaking with neighbors, talking with residents—I have phone numbers of block captains and phone numbers of neighbors. That's the real work. The mobilization is important and key, yet a lot of the building power work isn't going to be on the front page of a newspaper or going to happen by sharing photos on social media. It's going to be a lot of the behind-the-scenes grunt work. I really want to amplify that, even if the summer is quiet. The summer can have no actions but that doesn't mean that we're not building power and building strength as a collective.

What I will also share with other collectives trying to think through demands is to make sure that you have a diverse cadre of folks who are in the room and can provide input. I heard this from an organizer recently. She said: "Gabe, I don't care who's in the room as much as I care about the fact that they are all on point and thinking differently about what needs to happen." Sometimes we get into a phase of wanting to check boxes. It's one thing to check boxes but it's another thing to make sure that you have folks in the room who can speak to it authentically so that we're not tokenizing. We want to avoid tokenizing and work toward having authentic levels of inclusion on ideas. More importantly, find time and space to carry out the creation of a shared vision and demands.

On the front end, we sometimes get caught up in the "do ... do ... do." We're in the midst of action so we want to hit the streets. Yes, all that stuff is important, and it actually catalyzed the growth of our individual and collective relationships. Yet, allowing ourselves to split half the time on the action and half the time on building infrastructure can help remove some of the backlog of work we had to do this winter [2020–2021] in order to collectivize on some issues. I will close by saying this: make sure you have as much input as you can from community members and not only from activists.

**Flare:** This relates to the other question about the demands speaking to the localized, intersectional needs of Philadelphians. Take, for example, demand number two: cease the criminalization of Black Philadelphians. The day that they tear gassed 52nd Street was a hot day. It would have been a good day to open the windows. What a lot of people got that day was tear gas and not fresh air. Not that fresh air exists in Philadelphia if you consider the vast impact of environmental racism. On the surface level, it seems like [the demand] may only pertain to Black protesters and Black radicals, but it doesn't. If you return to that example of 52nd Street, one in four children in West Philadelphia have asthma. If you have breathing problems (and there's lots of high-risk elders in West Philadelphia), you could have easily been killed by this toxin spread by the Philadelphia Police Department (PPD). From another angle, Black women's bodies and reproductive health have always been policed—tear gas acts as an abortifacient. There are so many factors and angles of analysis that must be accounted for within crafting demands to strike back at the intertwined oppressions and daily aggressions faced in any community.

**YahNé:** I wanted to mention the impact that our demands had on the larger community.

It really changed the way that people approached their demands. We recaptured the language of abolition. We're certainly not alone, but [our labor] contributed to the refusal of an intentional state-oriented reframing and redirecting of our movement. There's much made about the insertion of the "defund" language, but Ajamu [Ajamu Baraka, National Organizer for the Black Alliance for Peace] was so excited about our collective's demands because it was the only space that he was hearing about that took it all the way to abolition.

Imagine if we were without this documented set of demands and our ability through our direct relationships with organizers in other countries doing this work. Imagine if we were without the pressing forward, the organizing, the actions, the interviews, and additional things that we shared around that time. Our radical language may have been able to be co-opted and the conversation on abolition overshadowed. Instead, right now, we're in a space where the language and discussion of abolition is a part of the mainstream conversation. We've contributed to that significantly—recapturing, restoring, and protecting the need for abolition to be elevated is an important goal that we must reach.

We understood the importance of collectivism. Our intention was absolutely to tap into the collective wisdom to the full extent that it exists. We didn't do that only through those organizations that are named in the collective or who participated in the crafting of the demands. As organizers, recognizing the fact that you are a part of a larger community, we already have these expansive relationships. We are all informing each other, and we need to be keeping that in mind, the truth that what we do impacts one another.

When people looked at us and said that what we were suggesting was out of the realm of what's possible, we could point to what the Minneapolis City Council were pushed to do, making a commitment to removing the police.[9] We are all informed and empowered by each other, and we have to be brave. You have to know that our ability to secure what we deserve absolutely puts the entire system at risk. It kills the system when we demand what we deserve. We are absolutely threatening those who are in power. Black liberation is considered the most dangerous threat, because it *is* the most dangerous threat to the United States of America. We have to be brave and willing to articulate those needs and requirements in order to share the vision and language that is required. Without fear. Without hesitation. Without compromise.

**Krystal:** I will say that one of the biggest things I've learned and appreciated from being a part of the Black Philly Radical Collective is that there is such power within coalition. I know that sounds basic as hell, but many of us have been talking in our various corners or wherever we're working from that a coming together of Black organizing in the city is necessary. We've talked about previous iterations from the not-so-distant past, but it is critical we remember that we remain disunited to our peril. If all we do moving forward is have a space for the different organizations that are part of the BPRC to update each other on what we're working on, that would still be a contribution. That's not what we're going to do, but I just want to emphasize how valuable collective, cooperative, collaborative organizing work remains to be. We cannot lose sight of that, despite the presence of a lot of things that have to do with the interplay of the state and the commodification of the movement. I want to make a case for organizing in collectives when it's possible. I want to make a case for having and cultivating alignment.

---

9. Ed note: Minneapolis' City Council vowed to defund and dismantle the police department. That pledge has since been challenged by reformist solutions.

One of the things that made our work able to move in the way that it did, on top of our past relationships, was having a clear track record of abolitionist practice and organizing work. We knew who to call because we saw each other doing the work. We didn't have to struggle around the possibility of abolition. This doesn't mean we didn't struggle around what abolition is and what it should be, but we weren't sitting up here debating whether abolition or radicalism should be included in the scope of our work. That's important. We can't have motherfuckers up in here talking about reform. It's not helpful.

Beyond that, cultivating deeper levels of alignment such as understanding what you do agree on and what you don't agree on is really important when coming together as a collective around this abolition fight. This is not a contract signed in blood that says, "We need to organize with each other for the rest of our lives." We can focus on this particular [campaign]—one that is a very important piece of a larger Black liberation struggle. We always said, as a precursor to mobilization, that understanding this [sole campaign] is NOT what will get us to liberation, yet this is a huge part. There's something helpful about having a defined mission.

I know we have discussed them as demands but I also want us to see them equally as a vision. Demands can imply that we're focused on the state. You know what I mean? Don't get me wrong. We're making appeals to the state but really most of what this document has been about is sharing a vision, inviting people to struggle with us around that vision, and having that vision guide our work. That is far more important than "demands." We're not a fucking vanguard here. We don't understand ourselves as some kind of vanguard that's going to bring Negroes to the promised land. I'm not dismissing vanguardism because it can be valuable in certain kinds of contexts, but the real reason I'm saying that is because we are really focused on building power in our communities.

A lot of the stuff y'all don't see is when we were on Locust Street.[10] The person to person, block to block work is actually far more important than the action that made the news. Especially in a moment where it's the spectacular forms of organizing that get all the attention, we've all

---

10. The 6100 block of Locust Street is where Walter Wallace Jr.'s family lived and where he was murdered by Philadelphia police on October 26, 2020.

been very clear that we're *community* organizers. Ultimately, if nobody in the hood hears the message, or wants to struggle with us around the message, then this whole thing is DOA [dead on arrival]. We're very clear that's where the work has always been and where it will always be.

# A Story of Resistance in Eight Objects: A Study of the Material Culture of the 2020 Uprising

Malkia Okech

The 2020 Black Uprising in Philadelphia was nothing short of historical and certain artifacts shed light on the struggle that occurred. This study is an attempt to tell a story of the Uprising, through a review of eight objects that played a part in it and honoring the context in which they were contributed. These objects—as a community archive—will further uphold the 2020 Uprising as a part of Philadelphia's cultural heritage and radical history. This project is a living archive, breathing life into the experience of those who participated in the Uprising for the future movements to come.

The "resistance objects"[1] were obtained from an open call for submissions in February and March 2021. Contributors submitted a form documenting context, information, and images of each object. These objects include: shirts worn by Up Against the Law Legal Collective; a bullhorn from Black Lives Matter Philadelphia; protest uniform of scholar-activist Krystal Strong; safety goggles; a medic's safety helmet; a protest sign from six-year-old Coltrane Love; a COVID-19 mask from activist, digital archivist, and videographer Sunny Singh; and a nail from the Rizzo statue. All objects were made, used, received, and found in pursuit of justice for George Floyd and all who were targeted by state-sanctioned violence during the summer of 2020.

---

1. I define "resistance objects" as artifacts of the changemakers who participated in the Uprising. I use this term because I hope it conveys a sense of activity, dynamism, and aliveness that is observed here in the historical context of the Uprising, yet can and will continue to be a tool for resistance for future rebellions (either these specific objects or objects like them).

These eight objects represent a broad range of items. Each object tells a distinct story about an event, location, or role within the actions. Together, they portray the large, complex, moving vehicle that an Uprising is and that the protests were.

**Let 'em know!**

Messaging brings a movement together. Ideas, actions, and words dance towards common goals: freedom, liberation, and justice. It is through collective action and efforts that concepts like #BlackLivesMatter are able to take life. Each of these objects remind us of the screams, shouts, chants, and lessons on justice conveyed through them.

### 1. PYLE bullhorn (figure 1)

A contribution from Black Lives Matter Philadelphia, the bullhorn is a quintessential symbol for struggle in the streets, and certainly the struggle of the summer 2020 Uprising. According to the contributor, it was used in at least twenty-five actions. What most comes to mind when I ponder this object is the public recital of the Black Philly Radical Collective (BPRC)'s "13 Demands." Booming through a bullhorn just like this one, representatives of BPRC rattled off a list of statements covering the social, political, and economic justices owed to Black Philadelphians.

A bullhorn doesn't just amplify noise, it holds a platform for uprisings and provides a guiding voice to collective efforts. The voice behind a bullhorn holds the energy. They are an emcee, a hype-person, a facilitator, and steward of the streets. This tool and statement of power was vital for the different actions, demonstrations, and gatherings of the 2020 Uprising.

### 2. "NO POLICE – BLM" protest sign (figure 2)

Another staple of any protest is a sign. This submission comes from six-year-old Coltrane Love, the youngest contributor to this collection, who attended protests with his parents Anyabwile and Shivon Love.

Signs forge beliefs that unify a movement. They are the bread and butter of protest. They are the ultimate, albeit sometimes impermanent, historical markers of movements, providing us with historical and political context about a cause and details about who we honor or hold accountable. Signs are as much a craft as they are a statement in their own right. Printed or handcrafted signs band people and movements together in message and purpose.

Coltrane's sign is cardboard, yarn, watercolor, and pen. It is simple in craft yet radiant and raucous in spirit; it speaks volumes. "No Police – BLM" is the ultimate summary of the summer of 2020's nationwide struggle. He put this sign together from scratch, by himself, and by his own volition. Signs like this one, from children as young as Coltrane, are enough to strike hope in the hearts of any activist. Children, elders, and everyone in between were out in the streets in the summer of 2020. It ushered in a new wave of activism that formed a harmonious ocean of rage, joy, love, and desire for freedom.

### 3. Protest pins (figures 3a and 3b)

Another contribution from BLM Philadelphia is a group of pins. The pins represent BLM Philly and the fight to Free Anthony ("Ant") Smith, who is currently a defendant in an Uprising-related case.[2] The pins are produced by Philly for REAL Justice.

Like other objects in this collection, pins have a history as protest paraphernalia. Buttons and pins fashioned on a jacket, shirt, backpack, or other item share movement messaging, solidarity, and affiliation. Using bright colors and bold slogans, pins like these are hard to miss.

The BLM pin is both an advocate and an identifier for the Movement for Black Lives. The Free Ant pin brings awareness to Anthony Smith's case and serves as a daily form of advocacy. Unlike signs, these wearable articles are fixtures of near-permanent dispatches for what is happening in the movement.

---

2. Anthony "Ant" Smith, a prominent educator, organizer, and leader in Philadelphia, was arrested on politically motivated charges as part of an effort to suppress the Black Lives Matter uprisings, and to undermine those with powerful voices calling for justice. On October 26, 2020, Anthony was arrested and taken from his home by federal officers based on his alleged involvement in the arson of a police vehicle during a Black Lives Matter protest in May 2020. If convicted, he will face a mandatory minimum of seven years in prison. A huge outpouring of community support mobilized to protest the arrest. Anthony has received more than seventy character letters attesting to his selflessness and dedication in serving his community. The school where he works and the organizations where he volunteers his time immediately released statements to express their support. A social media campaign focused on freeing Ant quickly gained national traction. Anthony was released pretrial and is on a location monitoring program until his court date. See Appendix, 105.

## Safety first

A lot of us weren't ready for May 30 or the days and weeks that followed. Neither was the Philadelphia Police Department (PPD), according to reports.[3] They ruthlessly gassed, sprayed, and flash-banged crowds, shoving people around like cattle. To fight for George Floyd was to fight against a murderous white supremacist system, and to be in the streets for George Floyd was also to fight for ourselves, our lives, our right to stand up for freedom.

Across the country, people who fought for justice in their own cities faced similar repercussions for daring to take a stand against oppression, braving tear gas, rubber bullets, and other despicable methods of "crowd control."[4] Some suffered life-threatening and permanent or life-altering injuries.[5]

A critical aspect of protest and uprising is safety. This selection of objects covers some of the peripheral roles and protective mechanisms that keep protesters safe when we are out in the streets. The coordination and strategy of those who keep us safe is thankless work. If we think of an uprising in terms of core and periphery—the core being the center of action, confrontation, march, or protest and the periphery being the support structures that help maintain the flow and safety of said action. The periphery may contain bikers and marshals who perform traffic control and keep watch to make sure cops or reactionaries don't mesh into the crowd. It is also where anyone can step out and find a snack or

---

3. Chris Palmer and Mike Newall, "Philly Police Were 'Simply Not Prepared' for George Floyd Protests, Review Finds," *The Philadelphia Inquirer*, https://www.inquirer.com/news/george-floyd-protests-philadelphia-report-jim-kenney-danielle-outlaw-20201223.html.

4. See, for example: Office of the Controller, "Independent Investigation Into the City of Philadelphia's Response to Civil Unrest," https://controller.phila.gov/philadelphia-audits/civil-unrest-response/; Kim Barker, Mike Baker, and Ali Watkins, "In City After City, Police Mishandled Black Lives Matter Protests," *The New York Times*, March 20, 2021, https://www.nytimes.com/2021/03/20/us/protests-policing-george-floyd.html; David A. Fahrenthold and Devlin Barrett, "Police Turn More Aggressive against Protesters and Bystanders Alike, Adding to Disorder," *Washington Post*, https://www.washingtonpost.com/politics/police-turn-more-aggressive-against-protesters-and-bystanders-alike-adding-to-violence-and-chaos/2020/05/31/588ad218-a32f-11ea-b619-3f9133bbb482_story.html; "US Crisis Monitor | ACLED," July 7, 2020, https://acleddata.com/special-projects/us-crisis-monitor/.

5. Meg Kelly, Joyce Sohyun Lee, and Jon Swaine, "Partially Blinded by Police: Video Evidence Undermines Official Accounts of Injuries at George Floyd Protests," July 14, 2020, *Washington Post*, https://www.washingtonpost.com/investigations/2020/07/14/george-floyd-protests-police-blinding/.

assistance from a mutual-aid group. The periphery is also a critical stage for safety and legal support.

### 4. Up Against the Law T-shirts (2) (figures 4a and 4b)

Attend any protest, certainly a major one, and it won't be hard to spot a member of Up Against the Law Legal Collective (UATL) in a bright T-shirt, keeping an eye on the situation. UATL is a volunteer group of legal observers. It has become a common practice in preparation for protests to share and retain their number: 484-758-0388. Best in permanent marker on an arm or leg, where you could easily spot it in the event you are "picked up" or detained, and it may be all you have to let people know where you are. It's not uncommon to run into a "protest mom" ready to arm you with their number. Maybe you have a mnemonic device, maybe a song, maybe you chant it with your friends. UATL is a critical resource.

In many instances where arrests are made, UATL helps gather any images or videos, collect witnesses, and provides an organized avenue for handling arrest. The group also provides advocacy for arrestees and becomes spokespeople for folks in custody. This is considered a part of jail support, or post-protest-arrest gatherings, where they are there to make sure you are fine on the inside, have supporters on the outside, and that everyone is abreast of the situation. They connect activists to pro bono legal representation, offer Know Your Rights training, and are public-facing opponents of state repression.

The UATL uniform, a bright orange or green T-shirt with their information and statement of purpose, heralds a brave servant of the Uprising. For their wearers, they carry the risk of being identified as a threat by law enforcement. But for us, they are a way to keep us safe, informed of our rights, all while keeping an eye on what is going down in the streets.

A critical part of protest infrastructure, both T-shirts loaned to this project needed to be handled with gloves as they were subjected to CS gas (2-Chlorobenzylidenemalononitrile), otherwise known as "tear gas."

### 5. Goggles (figures 5a and 5b)

On May 31, the PPD launched an occupation of West Philadelphia. The National Guard took the streets from about June 1 to 10, concentrating its presence around 52nd Street for much of this time. A main commercial corridor, 52nd Street is a dividing line between the predominantly Black community west of 52nd, where the occupation occurred, and the area east of 52nd street that is gentrified. Roving from street to street, they systematically unleashed tear gas on residential blocks, fumes entering the houses of residents, families, affecting children and elders. The radius of this chemical attack was a predominantly Black neighborhood.

When you are in proximity to tear gas, the burn hits your nose and eyes, making it difficult to breathe and see. It is incapacitating. When protestors and participants in the struggle caught onto this repressive strategy, they distributed goggles. People began to collect funds to distribute goggles widely to comrades, friends, and anyone who needed them.

This pair was one such donation. It speaks to a protestor's go-bag for the Uprising, which at its best would also include some medical supplies, water for flushing out eyes, and other such items to help care for people and keep them safe.

### 6. Medic helmet (figure 6)

The unsung hero of the 2020 Uprising is the street medic. Much like Up Against the Law and legal observers, street medics are self-selected, passionate individuals who dedicate themselves to the purpose of keeping everybody safe and healthy at a protest. Considering the violent and inhumane methods of the PPD, street medics are essential to the cause while also being targets of state repression.[6]

As people are injured, impaired, dehydrated or lost, they usually retreat to the protest periphery, where they can find a medic station or medic street team. The teams are prepared with food, water, and strategies to flush out burning eyes and treat wounds. It is terrifying and indispensable work. Additionally, social media and word of mouth on

---

6. There is footage of the PPD seizing and vandalizing medical supplies; some medics on the ground reported being sought out and arrested. This was while police were assaulting people with rubber bullets, batons, and other senseless violence. [See Wudan Yan, "Health Professionals Say Police Are Targeting Them at Protests," *Medium,* June 15, 2020, https://elemental.medium.com/health-professionals-say-police-are-targeting-them-at-protests-52419b716282.]

the street became a tool where basic medical tips (such as "how to flush out eyes properly") would be disseminated so that more people could assume the role when a medic wasn't available.

A helmet, like goggles, proves necessary in an uprising. Gas canisters, flash bombs, and other debris flying through the sky can result in unfortunate consequences as we saw reported throughout the summer.[7] Additionally, the bright yellow helmet with bright red medic symbol and spelled-out role makes the wearer easily identifiable and recognizable to someone requiring their services, which happened all too often in the volatile environment of the 2020 Uprising.

## 7. 676 mask (figure 7)

This object had many uses in the Uprisings. Firstly, it's a COVID-19 mask. The collection would be incomplete if it did not acknowledge how the Uprising took place amidst a global pandemic. At every event, COVID-19 protocols were encouraged and many participants wore and handed out masks and distributed hand sanitizer. And while right-wing pundits tried to claim that the protests were large, illegal, super-spreader events, no such thing happened.[8]

What also makes this object significant is that it was worn on I-676, or the Vine Street Expressway, on June 1, 2020, the third day of major actions. This mask is owned by Sunny Singh, an activist, digital archivist, and videographer who documented portions of the Uprising. It was here that protestors took the highway and were met by a militarized group of police who effectively trapped everyone and tear gassed the packed crowd. As people scrambled up the grass ramps and hoisted each other over the fences onto the streets, police officers shot rubber bullets and arrested many of those who couldn't face the climb or make it out in time. Protestors sat on the boiling highway ground, bound by twist-tie handcuffs, and were met with additional pepper spray. The scene was horrendous and footage quickly spread across the national news. Sunny

7. Rebecca Rhynhart, "Independent Investigation into the City of Philadelphia's Response to Civil Unrest," Office of the Controller, January 27, 2021, https://controller.phila.gov/philadelphia-audits/civil-unrest-response/.

8. Gregory Neyman and William Dalsey, "Black Lives Matter Protests and COVID-19 Cases: Relationship in Two Databases," *Journal of Public Health (Oxford, England)* 43(2): 225–227, https://doi.org/10.1093/pubmed/fdaa212.

Singh, who loaned this object, recalls being hit by a tear gas canister himself. His footage was used to reconstruct the horrific event in an investigative piece in *The New York Times*.[9]

## Living relic

This category has been designated for objects that may not have been actively utilized in the Uprising. Instead of having a use or purpose they still have a story to tell that provides historical context and makes a statement about the powers at play.

### 8. Rizzo nail (figure 8)

On May 30, smoke, haze, the smell of fumes, and the sweat, blood, and tears of thousands under a blazing sun came to a head around the Frank Rizzo statue in front of the municipal building in Center City. Ropes, flags, and fire engulfed the infamous and imposing statue of former Philadelphia mayor Frank Rizzo. Rizzo was a racist tyrant of a police commissioner and mayor who was politically active from 1968 to 1980. He continues to reign as an icon of white supremacy, as seen through the longevity of his likeness that has persevered for decades after his regime.

This nail was spotted on the southeast corner, approximately five to ten feet away from Rizzo as protestors struggled and shuffled the statue back and forth on its stubborn mantle. It was a living symbol of the institution of policing and violence against Black Philadelphians, and this action became an ultimate metaphor of self-determination as people climbed, stomped, threw fire, and tried to tug away this monument to white supremacy. The nail pictured is one living relic of this struggle that ultimately resulted in the statue's removal by the city a few days later.[10] It represents a culmination of a decades-long grassroots battle that we won and will never forget.

---

9. Christoph Koettl et al., "How the Philadelphia Police Tear-Gassed a Group of Trapped Protesters," *The New York Times*, June 25, 2020, https://www.nytimes.com/video/us/100000007174941/philadelphia-tear-gas-george-floyd-protests.html.

10. Robert Moran, "Frank Rizzo Statue Removed from Outside the Municipal Services Building in the Middle of the Night," *Philadelphia Inquirer*, June 3, 2020, https://www.inquirer.com/news/frank-rizzo-statue-philadelphia-removed-msb-plaza-george-floyd-protests-20200603.html.

**Towards a radical archaeology of protest**

Without assuming where the call for submissions would lead, I have considered the life of each object as it relates to the 2020 Uprising. These objects tell a story of method, strategy, hope, and belief. They each evoke the observations, accounts, and experiences of activists and participants on the ground. If an uprising is a sum of boisterous moving parts hurtling towards collective liberation, these objects were instrumental parts of the equation.

# One Drop Placebo

Ewuare Osayande

*for Harriet A. Washington*
*for Dr. Bill Jenkins*
*for Dr. Susan Moore*

Ours is not some putrid concoction of deceptions
contrived by a confederacy of hucksters

Our fret is not with science per se
We know full well
what's been done to us
in its name
by those enrobed in white

How we've been frankensteined in the laboratories of madmen
who measured our skulls after killing us
said we were soulless as they savaged us

Whose eureka came from rape
and boiled tortures in glass beakers
Our blood measured in quadroon one-drop segregations
Babies lab ratted by doctors whose names grace university halls

Our Black hides stretched under government microscopes
Bodies laced with disease like the blankets you gave the Shawnee

Do you really expect us
to forget Tuskegee?

You lied to them
Hundreds of men
Told them they were being treated

As you prescribed pills coated in contempt
So you could watch them suffer
Jotting down notes with the disdain of judges signing death warrants

And you wonder why we don't trust

Seeing one of us get shot in the arm
cheesing
Ain't gonna change none of that

Did we miss the memo?

Missed when you paid damages
and signed acts as acknowledgment
of injustices injected
in doses of desuetude
as more than apologies emptied
of the actuals to address what ails us

When what ails us most is you?

But that would be too much like right
too much like reparations

How is it that laws meant to protect
when applied to us
have the same effect as a placebo?

When doctors are known to ignore our pain
leave us wasting in hallways gasping for basic dignity
send us home even when we are doctors like them
Then claim us hostile as prognosis
as though we should suffer peacefully
die gracefully
like when we get shot in these streets
and left to rot for hours as roadkill

When the walls next door got more rights than our Black lives
Since when you care whether we live or die
Since when?

# Philly Artists and Photographers React and Reflect

Nilé Livingston, Corey Hariston, Koren Martin, Malkia Okech, Nick Massarelli, Matthew Early, Joe Piette

Koren Martin

Koren Martin

Koren Martin

Koren Martin

Corey Hariston

Joe Piette

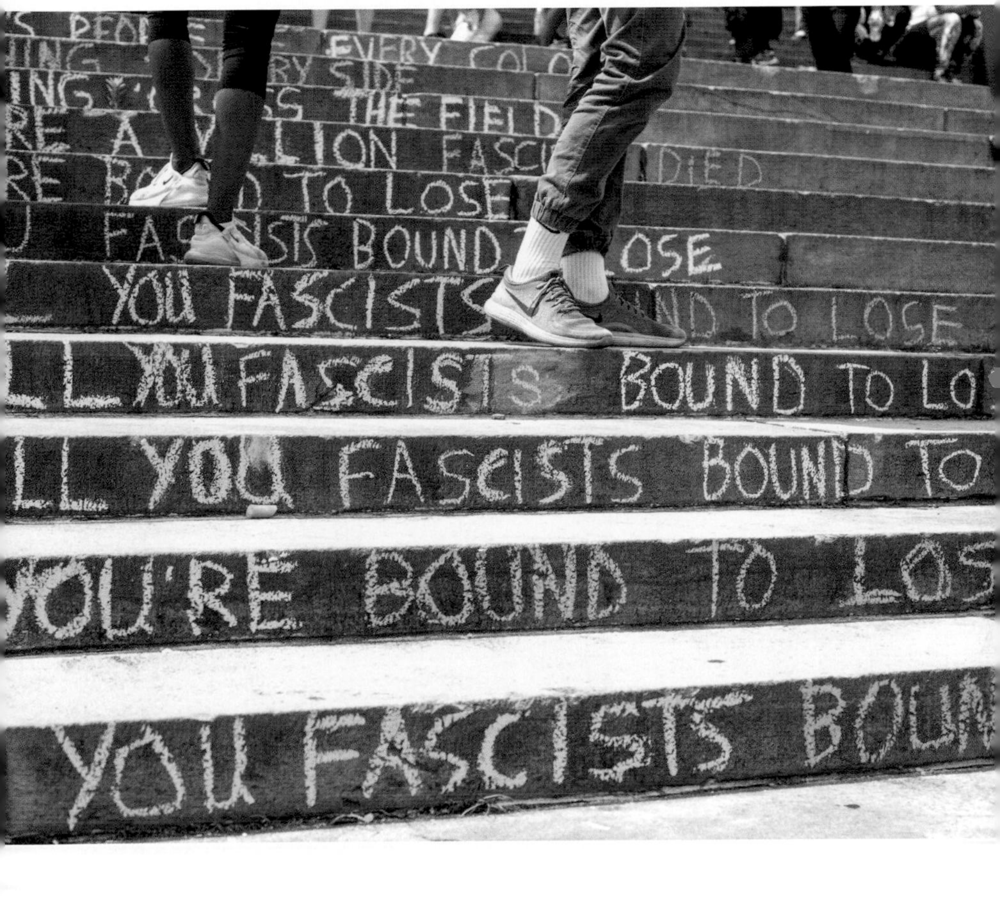
SIDE
THE FIELD
LION FASC
DIED
TO LOSE
BOUND
OSE
YOU FASCISTS
TO LOSE
YOU FASCISTS BOUND TO LO
YOU FASCISTS BOUND TO
YOU'RE BOUND TO LOS
YOU FASCISTS BOUN

# HAPPY
# BIRTHDAY
## DOMINIQUE "REM'MIE"
# FELLS

Commissioned by Meg Onli

Designed by Nick Massarelli

Printed by Matthew Neff
at Common Press

Reprinted with the
permission of Terri Edmonds

"It's My Birthday!" Dominique would always s this to her friends and loved ones, every ye Happy 28th Birthday Dominique "Rem'mie" Fe Dominique really only observed two holida Thanksgiving and her Birthday. This year, t WORLD celebrates the life of one of the m outgoing, caring, and vibrant souls to ever gra this Earth. Dominique was always one to give, matter what she had. This week you all have giv her the ability to give back one last time. Your ki donations will aid in the prosperity of the place t Dominique called a home away from home. behalf of Dominique, her family, and friends, Tha you. Thank you for giving a voice to the voicele and a chance to those who probably thought they already seen their last. Her spirit is shining brigh than ever today, tomorrow, and the day after th We will ALWAYS say her name. From the bottom our hearts, we love you Dominique "Rem'mie" Fe

Love,
Mommy, Dad, Desi, Dior & Family

# Hakim's Bookstore: Preserving Lifelong Missions, Instilling Knowledge-of-Self

Tafari Diop Robertson in conversation with Yvonne Blake and Cheryl David[1]

After a brief introduction of her unique relationship to Hakim's Bookstore, Tafari asks the bookstore's current owner, Yvonne Blake, and close friend and dedicated volunteer Cheryl David, to reflect on the Philadelphia Uprising of 2020 alongside the history of Hakim's Bookstore (210 South 52nd Street in West Philadelphia).

Hakim's Bookstore is one of the first places I visited when I arrived in Philly in 2019. As I entered, I was immediately greeted by a resonant "Peace & Love!" from Chris Arnold, the store's lead volunteer clerk, community outreach, social media savant, and youth mentor, among many other supportive roles he's taken on since a 2015 article alerted him of Hakim's potential closing. I too made a home of the store, regularly visiting throughout the week to buy books, chat with customers, and offer help to Chris and Ms. Yvonne, the store's owner and daughter to its namesake. Initially, this help consisted of me sitting stubbornly until an opportunity arose to prove my usefulness to this small bookstore family.

I didn't know anyone in Philadelphia at the time. I'd driven myself from Austin, Texas, where I was born and raised, in hopes that Philadelphia could be a fresh start for my adult life. Hakim's Bookstore was the first place to, perhaps reluctantly, take me in. Simply by existing as a warm, dedicated space for circulating Black knowledge, it became my first and most direct sense of what my Philadelphia community could be.

---

1. Excerpted and edited in collaboration with Christopher R. Rogers.

It is, in fact, a family, sustained by Ms. Yvonne and her close friends, Ms. Glenda and Ms. Cheryl David. They grew up in the store together. Glenda and Cheryl both worked at Hakim's since they were teenagers and have continued to support the store over the years. After the passing of her father, Ms. Yvonne took over the store with her own daughter and granddaughter, maintaining the family legacy. There hasn't always been such support for Black bookstores, so the dedication to keeping Hakim's alive is no small feat. Ms. Yvonne regularly laments the years when they were only able to open once a week, sustained by this small support system and income from Ms. Yvonne's other career.

Since the uprisings and attention spurred by the deaths of George Floyd Jr., Breonna Taylor, and other lives lost at the hands of police, business at Hakim's has surged. It is sad that these recent killings of Black people have been the catalyst for people to see the value in Black history, culture, and literature. So many other Black bookstores have not survived long enough to experience this surge in interest. They often close abruptly, unannounced, due to natural shifts in the limited support systems that keep them alive. Not only are family legacies lost in this process, detailed histories, feelings, and experiences of a community are also lost.

The following conversation is a testament to the energy preserved within Hakim's Bookstore, an intergenerational movement and ongoing legacy created in 1959 by Dawud Hakim, father of Yvonne Blake and founder of the bookstore. It's the oldest Black-owned bookstore in the United States.

**Tafari Diop Robertson: Could you tell us a bit of the history and what has sustained Hakim's Bookstore throughout all these years?**

**Ms. Yvonne Blake:** Stores like ours are necessary. They're actually a foundation because it seems like the institutions and the schools are not really interested in educating people about the accomplishments of African Americans, so we have to do it ourselves and the way to do that is to have your own stores and to educate your own children.

One of the quotes on our website is, "We're the only people that allow the oppressor to educate our children." So parents and individuals have to take a greater responsibility for learning their history and then going forward. Once my father learned that he was not a slave and that there were people that came before him that accomplished great things, that was it for him. This store became his dedication to that mission; to act, to fight for equal everything. We deserve the right to be here just like everyone else and we need to be acknowledged.

We're basically the same store since opening in 1959. Our mission and what he hoped to accomplish has never changed. It was not just to educate African Americans but everyone about African American history, to let us know that our history did not start with slavery. The only recent change is that there are now more books out there about racism. We sell books that we sold forty or fifty years ago, because history does not change. We emphasize that you can't know who you are unless you know where you've been and what has been omitted from the education system. Our store provides African Americans and the world a knowledge-of-self so that we know how to go forward. So we know that we have value. So we know we are much more than the way we've been portrayed in the media and by government agencies.

One thing about my father [Dawud Hakim] is that he never sought out recognition for what he was doing. That's something that I admired him for. He wasn't running around to the government. He wasn't running around to City Council and trying to get awards and things. He was just very humble in what he did, and he was just very dedicated and steadfast, and I respect him so much for that. He was one of the first people to ship books to the prisons and it became apparent to me how important that was because I have customers that come in here and tell me thing like, "When I got in trouble and went to prison, your father was sending me books," or "Hakim's Bookstore [is where] somebody in my family might've asked for a book and it got me to reading and I realized that I was on the wrong path." So many of these people are upstanding people. They got in trouble as young kids and they tell me what a force my father was as far as talking to the young men in the community and trying to get them to understand that they didn't need to be doing the things they were doing. They needed to get knowledge-of-self.

My foundation was in this bookstore when I was nine or ten years old. My father always tried to impress upon us what he was trying to do. My regret is I didn't realize the value, not only of what he was trying to do, but what he had accomplished and what he had to go through to accomplish that. Once I became aware, as I became an adult and had a better relationship with my dad, understanding what his goals and desires were, it just was automatically natural that I was going to take over this role and continue his legacy. When we knew he was not going to survive, that is what I promised him; that I would keep this store open for as long as I could. As I said, having been here and having talked to people who knew him, I realize that he accomplished a lot more than I ever gave him credit for and that he was a trailblazer in this area. So I'll do it as long as I can and then I hope to pass it down to my grandchildren and to my daughter.

**Tafari: What was it like during the uprising, especially the day of May 31 when 52nd Street burst into open rebellion?**

**Ms. Yvonne:** We were here, Chris [Arnold] and I were here packing up books, because when George Floyd was murdered we got flooded with mail orders all of a sudden. And so we got to be here because it's too much to do at home. So we were here and Chris Rogers from the Robeson House called to ask if we were okay. We didn't know anything was going on. And then I was like, "What are you talking about?" They said, "Well, you know, there's some things going on off of 52nd Street." Then we saw a lot of people congregating outside. Chris [Arnold] and I went to the door and the first thing I saw were two SWAT team trucks sitting out in the middle of 52nd and Walnut Street. And I'm like, what is going on here? And I've never seen the SWAT team like that. People were like, what are you going to do? I got out of here and I went home. I didn't know what was going to take place. I just knew that it was getting ugly and that what had happened to George Floyd was ugly. We were still reeling from that and that people weren't going to take it anymore. And it was frightening.

**Ms. Cheryl David:** They were relentless. It was nothing but time and opportunity. And I'm telling you! There were some older people out there too, but the younger generation led. They were making a point: "It's not going to be this way. We're not having it."

**Ms. Yvonne:** All this time I thought I was accepted, well, not me personally, that Black people were accepted. That we were on our way. That white people really were trying to work with us. And that wasn't true. I felt like a second-class citizen. I felt very demoralized when that happened. It's almost like I was living in a fairytale world and there was another world going on. And I don't like this real world. And it's very frustrating. Yeah. It makes you want to pack up and go away and just not do anything and not try to interact with people. I'm angry. I'm an angry senior citizen that doesn't feel that things are going the way they're supposed to be going and that it's not going to change in my lifetime.

Nobody could actually believe that this policeman was doing what he was doing, knew he was getting filmed while he was doing it, and that nobody could stop it. This was right in your face. This is right in your face. And I have said, you know, jokingly, I'm ready for the revolution. I'm kind of old here, but I'll go out there and march. I marched for Trayvon. You know, it's just, I'm at that point. I'm sick and tired of white supremacy. I'm sick and tired of just trying to prove that we deserve a place on this earth to be alive and to simply live our lives. That's all we want to do. Live our lives.

**Ms. Cheryl David:** It's interesting how things happen—when one thing happens, how it trickles and makes something else to happen. With this mayhem that we had gone through for the four years of the presidency of Donald Trump and what's still going on, it's made people more conscious. And I'll tell you what, the pivotal point wasn't just that it helped Hakim's Bookstore, but the people, the young people who were protesting every day brought the consciousness to people and many of the people who don't look like us. Their children were out there and this made them have to be conscious of what's going on, because the young people are relentless. They don't think the way we do. They're not going to behave the way we do. They're not going to accept the things that we have.

I've understood that, but I always say it's not one or the other. It's both of us. The young people still need the older people to help them navigate, you know, understand the lay of the land, who the players are and how to play the game. It's the young people who are vigilant and forcing the hands of people to look at things as they are because they're not going to live and accept the things that we did coming up. They're just not. They've never lived in that world and they're not planning to be in that world. So that's where we're at right now. I think there's a lot more Blacks realizing who they are, their power in realizing everything that we were born to be, and everything that [white supremacy] attempted to prevent us from recovering.

**Ms. Yvonne:** I guess I was thinking that there was a way out before the insurrection on January 6, 2021 at the Capitol in Washington, DC. That was just like another slap in the face. And to think that I live on a planet where there are people who think like those that were down there at the Capitol is frightening and disheartening again. And I don't know how to get past that. I don't know. I don't know what we're going to do. Education is a start. The young people are educating themselves. They're going to have to. There's going to have to be a change in school curriculum, what people are taught from a young age, and parents of all races are going to have to take responsibility for making sure that their children know. Well, it's kind of hard if you don't actually believe that other races and minorities are equal to you, then it's hard for you to teach that to your children. So, I guess that's why it's going to have to take place in the school and hope that it sticks and that the influence, whatever negative influences are in the home, don't overshadow or overpower the facts, because African American history is American history and they are facts. It is not just a story. But, if you've got parents that are not going to encourage you, then at some point in time you're going to have to make the decision as to what kind of world you want to live in and whether you want to live in ignorance and hate and fear or accept that other people have value and have something to bring to the table.

# Goin Home Suite: Finding Hope, Wellness, and Freedom

Gabriel Bryant

## "Goin Home" Revisited

The beat for "Goin Home" was the first one producer and DJ Oluwafemi (Femi)[1] sent me when I asked him for production for an EP I wanted to make. It was April of 2020, and the world was in the throes of COVID–19. My father had just come home from being hospitalized with the novel coronavirus and I knew that I wanted to document this period through hip hop. My initial idea was to make an album speaking to the myriad emotions that enveloped that moment—the pain, loss, despair. I began framing ideas as I always do with any new production: writing down thoughts and lines as they came to me throughout the day. As the beats continued to come, I felt great about what this EP could turn into.

Then May 25 happened and everything changed. That week saw the murder of George Floyd, rebellion in Minneapolis by the following day, and an uprising in Philly by the weekend. It prompted me to send Femi a message via text: "The nature and content of this album just changed, bruh."

Even as I shifted the ideas for the songs that framed the rest of the project, the feelings that the beat for "Goin Home" gave me remained

---

1. Oluwafemi is a deejay, music producer, and visual artist based in Philadelphia, by way of Central New Jersey, by way of Lagos, Nigeria. He is inspired by drums and patterns and the rhythmic evolution of repetition. For over a decade, Oluwafemi has enjoyed mixing songs of drum-influenced genres—the family of funk, hip-hop, soul, reggae, dancehall, house music, and their countless offshoots. To learn more, see his Instagram page, https://www.instagram.com/olwfm/.

the same. The tempo, hard-hitting drums, and sample gave me vibes ripe to tell a story. Or maybe a couple of stories. At the time, local activists and organizers were rallying to support the annual campaign of the Philadelphia Community Bail Fund—an entity I helped to organize in its early years—and the work of the Mama's Day Bailout, an effort launched in 2017 to amplify the need to "Free Black Mamas" and bail out mothers and caregivers from jail. This experience would essentially set the tone for the first verse of the song. The cries to defund the police, to abolish the police—hallmarks of the 2020 summer protests—also informed the lyrics.

As a long-time organizer with Mobilization4Mumia, the Campaign to Bring Mumia Home, and a MOVE supporter, I have witnessed the tragic outcomes of mass incarceration up close and personal. The tentacles of white supremacy and anti-Blackness have a firm grip on a justice system that is in fact, criminal, with Black and Brown folks suffering in its traps every day. Ending this scourge on my people has become more than some volunteering, or even work, but truly a calling.

Active in the field of behavioral health, I also saw firsthand the mental health challenges that people were having as the world shut down around them, including those who found themselves working from home. Though many acclimated fairly quickly, for others, the excitement that came from a morning commute turned into daily, dreadful mornings; the fresh air and recharge that came from walking to lunch or during breaks turned into slow walks to the kitchen and being trapped by the same four walls for hours on end. It was claustrophobic, suffocating, and depressing.

I thought of a concept that could be developed by merging these two seemingly different experiences onto one track. I was playing the beat in the kitchen while writing one day when I began mumbling to myself, "I'm goin home, I'm goin home . . ." over and over. It just came to me. I then found a way to connect the first-person perspective of a man who was locked up and released from jail with the view of someone struggling with the perpetual Zoom meetings for work and how he would escape that difficult space through familial support and the beauty of Black literature.

I desired the following for listeners as they heard the song: that they would be moved to join an organization; support folks who are locked away in prisons; donate to organizations like the Philadelphia Community Bail Fund; prioritize their mental health and emotional well-being; and never forget the rich canon of Black authors who have historically provided joy, edification, uplift, and healing with their timeless brilliance and mastery of the written word.

It was only fitting that "Goin Home" would become track five on an EP I would call *RESTORATION*, because whether it is someone who exists on the margins due to imprisonment or someone suffering with their mental wellness, their full lives and spirit can be restored and, in the end, there's hope.[2]

## Lyrics to Goin Home

[3x]
I'm goin home
I'm goin home
I'm goin home
Yup, I'm goin home

Just got the word, received the notice
Said I'm outta here, so it's time to focus
Ain't asking no questions, or thinking 'bout motives
My celly put me on, said it's about COVID
Taking both of us, cause OG got sick
TV news came, now the plot's thick
All I know is, no more cold showers
No more cold meals and days-old chowders
I could taste freedom, I could feel power
Bout to be the slowest, 48 hours
Done living life, in a six by eight
Gonna run to my children, I can't wait
Devil parole board, used to fail son
In the yard, found out it was a bail fund

---

2. *RESTORATION* was released on January 9, 2021. Partial proceeds from this project have gone toward organizations working to free political prisoners and release vulnerable populations from prison due to COVID-19. The EP can be purchased on Bandcamp, https://gabrielprosser.bandcamp.com/album/restoration.

I'm done as the abuser, done as the booster
CO is my past, CEO is my future

So much time, so much time, cause I'm working from home
I'm a grind, I'm a grind, cause I'm here all alone
So many Zooms, breakout rooms, I stay at my computer
At 5, if I'm alive, then I'm in a stupor
Losing sight of my life, each day's like the last
Feeling stressed and depressed, always ready to crash
Dad called and I bawled, feeling just like a fool
Calmed me down, came around, started dropping some jewels
Said look, brought some books, man, these are our stories
We approached Mosley and Coates, these are our glories
Read 'em before, but for sure, now it is different
On Audible, was affordable, and now I am listening
Tapped the source on this pause, spirit deployed
Ntozake, Giovanni, be bringing me joy
Zora Neale, as Lauryn Hill sing in the background
And I'm all in, this Baldwin, guess I'm back now

[3x]
I'm goin home
I'm goin home
I'm goin home
Yup, I'm goin home

I'm goin home
I'm goin home
I'm goin home
I'm home

# Finding Freedom Inside the Cages: Interview with Robert Saleem Holbrook

Gabriel Bryant in conversation with Robert Saleem Holbrook

The following is excerpted from an interview between organizer and activist Gabriel Bryant and Robert Saleem Holbrook, Executive Director of the Abolitionist Law Center and cofounder and Coordinating Committee member of the Human Rights Coalition. The interview took place to correspond with the importance of inside/outside organizing that took place during 2020, as it was one of the major themes of Goin Home.

**Gabriel Bryant: What are some of the critical steps that organizers need to take to build on inside-outside organizing?**

**Robert Saleem Holbrook:** I think the first step would be connecting with people on the inside and their families on the outside, who are doing the day-to-day groundwork—not just to free their loved ones from prison, but also to protect them while they're still in prison. It's really important that, as abolitionists, and I'm just speaking to some people who may have that general political posture [others who self-identify as abolitionists] that it's important to struggle to abolish prisons. Also, until we abolish prisons, it's necessary—it's mandatory—that we fight for prisoners that are inside right now. Make sure that their dignity is respected, their humanity is respected, their lives are respected, and more importantly, that we can get them out of the beast, we can get them out of the jaws of the beast right now. And not just wait 'til this future that we are fighting for without prisons.

So in Philadelphia, that contact would be the Human Rights Coalition (HRC), which advocates on behalf of prisoners and their families to protect them while they are in prison, but also to abolish prisons. It's an abolitionist organization that was founded by political prisoners and politicized prisoners. Prisoners who were inspired and mentored by political prisoners like Russell "Maroon" Shoatz, Joseph "Jo-Jo" Bowen, Arthur "Cetewayo" Johnson. I was one of those younger prisoners that they mentored, and we set up organizations like the Human Rights Coalition to be a voice for prisoners, to fight for our liberation and freedom, but more importantly, to fight for the liberation and freedom of our people in this country.

**Gabriel: What specific tactics have actually been effective, whether it was with HRC or CADBI (Coalition Against Death by Incarceration), in the organizing work for the freedom of these people?**

**Robert:** The best tactics are when an organization or a movement is working in tandem with not just the prisoners on the inside, but their families and activists on the outside. More importantly, that we are involving prisoners on the inside, as our inside people. We are involving them in leadership decisions and we're also politicizing each other, because a lot of these families and even prisoners when they first come in, they're coming in pretty much from a place of self-interest. One fundamental thing: I want to get my loved one out of prison or I want to get out of prison. As activists, it's our job to politicize them, to show them that what's happening to you and your loved one is not happening in a silo and is not an anomaly. You are being oppressed by a criminal justice system that is doing exactly what it was designed to do—to destroy our communities and imprison our people. So, we have to engage in a political education process with families and prisoners. And the way that this is done is through the work, so that's done by direct action against the prison system. For example, if a prisoner is being abused, making sure that families get together and do a call-in to the prisons. That they do a rally outside of a prison, but more importantly, that they start contacting the prison authorities and saying that we're not going to tolerate this. They can start contacting politicians. They can start mobilizing the community around ending prison abuse, and more importantly, prisons don't work. That's one of the real messages we want to get across.

Family members are the perfect vehicle for that because they know it doesn't work, because they see their loved one in prison for decades, but they also see the harm that is continuing to happen in our community, harm that also impacts them. Thus, as I like to say—or as we like to say—there's no wall between victims and offenders in our community. By involving the family members and the prison in this, we're building a larger movement. By bringing families and prisoners into the movement, it politicizes them to understand that prisons in the United States are not an anomaly, they are doing exactly what they were designed to do, but also the larger problem is the United States. We need a fundamental change in this country.

So, we're bringing together prisoners and their families—groups that were marginalized from power—and now we have them talking about, what do we have to do to change power and to take power in this country? So, it's a political process as well as a process to support families and their loved ones in prison. That has been really effective for us. One thing I've learned is you empower people, that's how you bring about change. People feel empowered to make change. We've taken family members who were feeling alone, who were feeling isolated, who were feeling ashamed, who were feeling oppressed, and we connected them with other family members who were feeling the same way. When those family members are in the same room and realize that they are not alone, they find their strength, they find their voice, and they find their power.

**Gabriel: What keeps you hopeful?**

**Robert:** It's not a question of what keeps me hopeful, it's a question of what motivates me. And what motivates me is that I am part of a historic movement. I am connected to the legacy of a movement—the Black Liberation Movement. I am a part of this movement that has fought for generations and will continue to fight until our people are free. I'm standing on the shoulders of giants of the Black Radical Tradition.[1] I know that my legacy, my work, is directly connected to the work of

---

1. Cedric J. Robinson, Robin D. G. Kelley, Tiffany Willoughby-Herard, and Damien M. Sojoyner. 2021. *Black Marxism, Revised and Updated Third Edition: the Making of the Black Radical Tradition* (Chapel Hill: University of North Carolina Press).

George Jackson, Assata Shakur, Malcolm X. We could even go back to Nat Turner and to Harriet Tubman. We can go back to Octavius Catto here in Philly. That is what motivates me: I'm part of this rich, deep, Black liberation tradition and legacy. So, for me, it's not a question of what keeps me hopeful, it's a question of what is continuing to motivate me and fuel my fire.

Saleem encourages folks to get involved with the Human Rights Coalition (www.hrcoalition.org) and to contact them at info@hrcoalition.org.

# Greatest Love of All: A Meditation on Loving and Losing Black Women while Maintaining Strength in the Movement

Jeannine Cook and Youth Conductors of Harriett's Bookstore

I want to start off with a dedication to my Sisters—Sister Whitney, Sister Linda, Sister Breonna, and to my little Sisters Jen, Bri, and Ye, whose musings frame this collage of an essay. For all of my Sisters, I give thanks.

"We are still under attack," I remember thinking as my sister sends me a link to a news article about Breonna Taylor's murder. It is a hot gray morning in May 2020. Multiple people have shared the story with me at this point. "She was in bed, Jeannine," my sister says through sobs. "Sleeping, I know. I know," I respond. I think I know how to process this fuck shit or distract myself from processing this fuck shit. Music will help me, I guess.

Whitney Houston plays on the radio, singing "The Greatest Love of All," which only makes me feel worse. I turn it off. A year later, I still feel Breonna's grief in waves. Mostly in the mornings. Feeling that grip at the back of my eye sockets. Plotting out mood-settling techniques. Naturally, I am mourning, but not consciously, it is a more deep-in-my-spirit type of mourning, a heaviness like fatty deposits that live in my blood vessels. It does not stay, but when it hits, it is an attack. "We are still under attack," I type in the notes section of my phone.

I am a shopkeeper at Harriett's, an independent bookstore in the Fishtown section of Philadelphia. In the shop, I train groups of Youth Conductors—who I lovingly call our interns—to be community leaders under the guiding light of Harriett Tubman. Most of our Youth Conductors are Black girls. Tell me, how do you listen to the confusion and sadness in a Black girl's voice when she shares her version of Breonna Taylor's life with you? When do you explain state-sanctioned lynching to this dear child? How do you put this murder into a historical perspective? When do you tell her that she is under attack?

"You give her an outlet," an ancient voice whispers in my left ear. "Don't be afraid to take her to the frontlines and let her lead the way," the ancient voice says in my subconscious mind. So, I do. I'd gone to Minneapolis to give out books to organizers protesting the murder of George Floyd a few weeks earlier. We'd given out books here on the streets of Philadelphia. It felt completely imbalanced not to travel to Louisville to do something on behalf of Breonna Taylor.

I took the Youth Conductors with me. We flew to Kentucky to read to children in Injustice Park and distribute free books to parents. When we arrived, we were surrounded by militarized police officers and snipers on roofs. Of course, story time was canceled, but our mission to celebrate women authors, artists, and activists continued. We gave away all we had. Our Youth Conductors stood in front of hundreds of organizers, protestors, and police chanting "free books!" and "knowledge is power!" as they handed out copies of *Building a Movement to End the New Jim Crow: The Organizing Skills Guide*. We gave away everything we had, and when the Youth Conductors were ready, we left. That night we sat silent, listening to the shooting outside. We found out later that one person was killed, and multiple people were injured in the park a few hours after we'd left. "We are still under attack," I say to myself on the plane leaving Kentucky. Jen, who is one of our Youth Conductors and twelve years old, had this to say about the experience:

> We went to a protest for the death of Breonna Taylor in Louisville, Kentucky. At the protest, when we first got there, we saw a bunch of cops with huge guns looking at everyone. The whole thing was divided with the cops in the streets at a gate, almost as if they were trying to hold back the protesters. I was scared to walk in the streets because of the police, but me and Bri [another Youth Conductor] got the books and we passed them out to each and every person. Everyone there was so kind and thankful for the pins and books we gave out. Being at the protest I learned the importance of fighting for a cause despite people that stand in your way.

It's been a year since our visit to Louisville. I am sitting outside under the rays of a new spring sun, thinking about what to write for this submission, and *The Greatest Love of All* by Whitney Houston comes on again. And, sure, maybe it was a coincidence, but I'll take in the lyrics this time. That same ancient voice says once again, "You give them an outlet."

So here at the frontlines of this essay are the youth's words as an outlet and another chance for them to lead the way. And while I am humming the lyrics to the song, it occurs to me just what happened to Whitney Houston. And what it means to lose a Sister so publicly. And, how many of us mourned Whitney and how many of us still do? What does it mean to exalt our Sisters' names in their deaths and how do we memorialize their legacy for generations to come? This woman gave society, our culture, many cultures, all she had, and all the Youth Conductors know about is her tragic death. So I play "The Greatest Love of All" for them on repeat and sing the lyrics aloud to remind them that they are loved. I text them the lyrics and ask them to memorize so they, too, sing along. Like Whitney Houston sang, I, too, believe the children are our future. This is evident in how the Youth Conductors encountered and processed the experience of Breonna's killing and our role in the protests that followed. The following is shared by Bri, a seventeen-year-old Youth Conductor:

> Going to Louisville, Kentucky was one of the most remarkable experiences that I've ever encountered. Being that Louisville was my first time ever going to the South, it was definitely a culture shock. Everything—from the food, the people, and the environment— gave me a new perspective. Walking into the protest, I could feel a different energy. The police stood in formation on the street, firearms in hands, ready for anything as the civilians stood and chanted closer to the sidewalk. There were countless signs along the curb vocalizing the frustration felt in the air.
>
> When I first heard about Breonna Taylor, I was nauseated. The fact that people could do such a thing with no reason or remorse was appalling to me. Standing in the exact place where Breonna Taylor was blatantly murdered only made me realize the power that we have. The impact that we can make on the system and the influence

that we hold over our brothers and sisters. Only then did I truly comprehend my role in the many protests that I've participated in as a Harriett's Bookshop Youth Conductor. We must educate ourselves and share the knowledge that is bestowed upon us. We must use these times as an opportunity to better ourselves and the next generation. As I learn that STILL, no one is being held accountable for Breonna Taylor's death, it only makes me want to fight more.

"The Greatest Love of All" was written by a woman named Linda Creed from right here in Philadelphia. She wrote the song from her deathbed as she was battling breast cancer. She attended Germantown High School and penned multiple classics for the Sound of Philadelphia.[1] I tell the Youth Conductors that the song's Philly roots explain its raw realness. Linda died just before the release and major success of Whitney Houston's rendition of her song. But, my dear Linda, your legacy lives on. This verse reminds me of Breonna Taylor and the current state of activism. And about state-sanctioned lynching. And about the co-opting of movements. And I imagine what it would look like if we dedicated time to mourn and repair harm properly. And I remember the first day that I told the Youth Conductors to take to the streets with books instead of signs reading "I Can't Breathe." And how we went back and forth about it, but in the end, they listened to me, and now we've distributed a few thousand books. All because that is all that we had. And how sometimes we find ourselves seeking a hero to do activism on our behalf when, we are the only ones who can fulfill our needs. Sixteen-year-old Ye Ye had this to say:

> As an intern at Harriett's Bookshop, I am educated and aware of what is needed of me in order to alter the world and create social change. I am a biracial female born in a Latin household. Prior to being an intern, I was insecure of the African features bestowed upon me. I desired the Latin features that were concealed. When discussing this problem with Jeannine and participating in the various events at the bookshop, I gained an understanding that African features are something to display with confidence. Through

1. See The Sound of Philadelphia (TSOP), https://en.wikipedia.org/wiki/TSOP_(The_Sound_of_Philadelphia).

understanding this, I was capable of advocating for social change because I knew that I was not the only biracial female who felt this way. Society targets anything associated with African Americans, and Harriett's allowed me to understand that. On another occasion, a song titled *Can't Breathe* was presented to the 9/10 Choir at my school. The song focused on the issue of police brutality towards the minority, but it was in the perspective of the minority. The majority of the 9/10 Choir is of European descent, resulting in me feeling uncomfortable to hear people who do not deal with these hardships state "I Can't Breathe." I felt disgusted. When I informed Harriett's team of this problem, I felt supported. They informed me on how to deal with this disagreement. I discussed the issue with a choir teacher, and after a few months, the song was removed from the 9/10 Choir.

Society attempts to ensure that people of African descent are quiet, but I will not please society's expectations of me. As a Youth Conductor, I am no longer silenced. I have gained a different perspective of being a person of African descent. I will continue to advocate and fight for a change.

To the Youth Conductors who boldly stood on the frontlines of many protests beside me, who follow in Harriett's footsteps beside me, and whose words live on in this anthology beside mine, remember that even though we are still under attack, you are the greatest counterattack. You have the right and the responsibility to lead the way, to live as you believe, and to find your strength in love. *Ase*.

# Mobilizing the Digital Community

Rasheed Ajamu in conversation with Stephanie D. Keene and
Dr. Nina Johnson

The *Phreedom Jawn* Instagram page came into being in 2020 as a
response to heavy police and state presence in Philadelphia. I started
and run this page on the premise that I am not *the* community, I
am *a part* of the community and continue to use the page as a
dissemination tool, engaging folks invested and interested in the work
of Black liberation. Over the summer of 2020, the *Phreedom Jawn* and
social media became a crucial tool in mobilizing, aiding, and engaging
Philadelphians across the city and in that I learned ways to expand
and deepen the work of digital organizing and mobilization.

To discuss this work, I reached out to two people who have interacted
with the *Phreedom Jawn* page and have been doing movement work
in Philadelphia for years. Those folks are abolitionist and creator
Stephanie D. Keene and Swarthmore Sociology and Black Studies
professor Dr. Nina Johnson. We discussed how we came to know
each other, how social media has impacted movement work, and how
the @*PhreedomJawn* community and social media at large aided in
the Uprising of summer 2020 and the greater conversations around
abolition. What follows is not the entirety of our discussion, but I hope
it resonates with those who read these words.

**Rasheed Ajamu: I want to start off by asking you both—what
work do you do?**

**Stephanie Keene:** First, thank you. Thank you for inviting us, thank
you for having us, thank you for asking us, thank you for your work. I

think it's best that we not mention the group that Nina and I are both a part of by name . . . but that's actually how we met. We're members of a collective of educators, scholars, writers, and artists who are both incarcerated and non-incarcerated individuals who work together to educate people about prison systems, about education systems, about how these systems influence each other. We're very intentional about doing our work in relationship and always checking to make sure that it has the intentions and integrity that we talk about, right? I feel like a lot of times folks talk about work in a particular way, but then they practice work in a different way.

**Nina Johnson:** So what work do I do? I'm a teacher. I'm also in that collective and I'm a researcher. I'm a daughter, sister, aunt, partner, friend, and community member. I see my role as, in addition to being a teacher and a researcher, really moving resources from resource-rich places to places that have lots of ideas and lots of intellectual capacity, but not always the sort of economic, political, and social resources to do more of what they need to do. I think that's a really important thing to be doing when you have access to spaces. I really see that as my job. I don't really see much more I need to do at a white capitalist institution like Swarthmore than move resources from Swarthmore to other places.

**Stephanie:** And that's a beautiful thing.

**Rasheed: When was the first time you connected with the *Phreedom Jawn* page and how did you actually come across it?**

**Stephanie:** I came across it because I already followed you on Twitter before the name change. I don't remember how I found you there but I think you posted on Twitter about the Instagram page and I followed it. At the time, your Twitter account was more of a personal page. So I like to say that I was one of the "day ones."

**Nina:** The students at Swarthmore always ask me, "How do I . . . ?" They always email me about anything social media related. They think I know everything. And I'm always like, "Ask Stephanie; I don't know, Stephanie knows." Stephanie had posted something from the *Phreedom Jawn* page, and I said, "Well, here's some good information, follow this person about the housing encampments [on the Parkway] because they wanted to bring stuff down." And then you [Rasheed] posted, "This is what people need. Don't bring it on this day. Don't show up here." And I realized, "Oh, this is such good information." I thought it was very ethical the way you spoke about the issues, the information you chose to share, and how you shared it. That really stuck out to me. But then it was also Rem'mie Fells—the way you spoke about her death and the need for us to care about the lives of people, not just what happens to them in death. I thought that was really important. Also, you are funny and your captions are humorous. I'm always trying to tell my students to choose joy and that the reason our revolutionary practices or our work for justice or liberation isn't attractive to people is because we (appear) joyless.

**Rasheed: How have you seen your abolition work represented on the *Phreedom Jawn* page or social media at large? How so or why not?**

**Stephanie:** I think the way Nina said it was beautiful and accurate. I think the things that you post and the way that you post are, if I hadn't known you before following the page, I would have said, "Oh, these are my folks. This is my kind of carrying on."

That and the way that you handled the vaccination scam [Philly Fighting Covid].[1] You've done it a couple of times. Anytime you posted something that you found out was not legit, was the wrong information, or was problematic in some way, you come back and you're offering "Here's what I did from a good place and good faith and it turned out not to be X, Y, Z, or whatever." I just appreciate that transparency.

Did I speak about work? It's a page that I feel comfortable sending people to without having to give any sort of caveat or check what's on the page before I send somebody over there. You were the first person I saw a post about the vaccine scam, but if you hadn't been—and if

---

1. Max Marin, Nina Feldman, Alan Yu, "Philly Fighting COVID kicked out of city vaccine program after sudden switch to for-profit," *WHYY*, January 25, 2021, https://whyy.org/articles/philly-fighting-covid-kicked-out-of-city-vaccine-program-after-sudden-switch-to-for-profit/.

somebody else had posted it—I would have then come to your page to see what the latest info was. There's a level of accuracy and due diligence to your work that I don't often see reflected in social media at large. I don't know how you've managed to do anything else when the page is updated. It feels very aligned with the things that I do, the things that I'm interested in, and the things that I want to know about.

**Rasheed: Both of you brought up the idea of transparency. Can you just explain why transparency is very important specifically in this kind of atmosphere—the digital realm—when it comes to movement work and mutual aid and different things like that?**

Nina: Well, I would say there's a lot of disinformation and misinformation circulating, and I don't know if it's just in digital spaces or on the Internet, but just broadly, to Black people about Black people. Part of loving us is being honest and I just think that if you don't have trust, we don't have much. Trust is the cornerstone of any relationship, and if we don't have a relationship we don't have anything.

Transparency and honesty is very important. That care ethic, that love that's at the basis of everything you do is everything for me. If you don't love Black people, then you don't really want us to be free. And so, we're not on the same project if you don't love us and love all of us, exactly how and where we are. And I think that really comes through; I think the fierce protectiveness that you have over Black people in all different kinds of ways is really important, but also the correction—the "this is not cool, this is not right. And we're not gonna uphold this in this space"—is also love.

I think all of those things are what constitute a relationship of love and a way of treating a relationship. And if you dishonor your relationship with those who follow you, then you are not about liberation, you are not about this work. For me, transparency is everything. I think people need to see us be vulnerable, humble, teachable, and evolving. Because I think the notion on social media is that there is some perfect face to present and that is just wrong.

**Rasheed: The Uprising of summer 2020 was one of the most major expressions of a collective spirit of liberation and of being free that we've seen in Philadelphia. Can you describe what y'all made of the 2020 Uprising and how did it make you feel?**

**Nina:** Nervous. It made me feel really nervous. I'll say that first because it was a pandemic. I was a little bit nervous about that in terms of there being so many Black people out there and Black people already not having access to good healthcare and treatment. I was also heartened because of my students who are young and they really have a heart for Black people. They really have a heart for liberation. They're really honest and they're really sincere, and I think they're so disappointed all the time because they want more people to care and they want more people to jump in. So, I think they were really heartened to see how many people cared.

Now, they don't trust any white person ever. I don't know where these kids came from but they really don't trust white people. So, they really didn't care for the white people being out there.

**Stephanie:** I was also nervous and I was really angry that we were being made to choose between being vocal and visible *and* being healthy and safe.

But when I was there, one thing was different for me. Often our actions, at least in Philly, are in Center City or at some city building or landmark. Which serves a purpose. But the actions that I went to were all in West Philly and I felt it was just so different to see people out on their front porches cheering us on or thanking us or joining us. Walking down their front steps and joining the march. That to me was so impactful because it wasn't abstract. Sometimes we can get inaccessible in our actions.

**Nina:** I think that the key for me too is that we can get lulled into believing if we just get a better person into this position, in this institution, things will change. And I think Larry Krasner proved that he is a prosecutor and is interested in upholding the system because he sent more children into the system and into facilities during a pandemic.

And so in 2020, we said we're going to be about ending this thing, 'cause there's no kinder, gentler system by which people can be unhoused.

There's no kinder, gentler system putting people in shelters. There's no kinder, gentler system in which we can incarcerate people. What the State of Pennsylvania and our city's prosecutor did is to sentence people to death. So, either we're going to really root this out and deal with it or we're not. We're in a moment where not dealing with it and opting for the kinder, gentler option leads to death. I was really heartened to hear people saying "Defund the Police" and "Abolish the Police." That's not something we often hear in the public sphere. There are some voices here and there, but I was really saying, "Yes, let's do this thing. I am with y'all, I am in this."

**Rasheed: How have you seen social media contribute to the 2020 Uprising? How effective do you think it is in mobilizing folks?**

**Nina:** The way I have always preferred to communicate and organize is face to face. COVID made that impossible. Social media became the place to gather, share information, strategize, and plan. I was not a user of social media before the pandemic. What I think social media, and the public sphere more broadly allows, is for our folks—those without the backing of corporate media or the sanction of the state—to narrate their own experiences, share their knowledge, and circulate their stories. Once we have a clear sense of what is happening here, we can work together on how we go about addressing it and making the world we envision for ourselves. Social media allows us to know what we otherwise would not, to see what those in power would keep hidden from us, and to think, organize, and act collectively. It was critical in 2020.

**Rasheed: There tends to be a lot of gatekeeping when it comes to the sharing of information. Can you describe why it is essential to make information accessible and how activists and organizers can spread it?**

**Stephanie:** I think it's important to make information accessible because the withholding of information is how we are marginalized and oppressed. It's not the only way but it's a big part of it. So, I'm thinking about job postings. Fortunately, I'm comfortable enough at the moment that I can refuse to apply for a job if they don't post salary information.

But I remember not being that comfortable and having to go through this process of figuring out what y'all are paying for this job. A lot of employers have gotten better and are super-transparent, but a lot of them are not. I use that as an example of: you're not being upfront about the salary because then you can find out I'm a Black woman and pay me less. That's why it's important to be transparent, and I think in the context of social media platforms, it's so that people can get resources to where they need to go. I think you are able to get resources to people because you have been transparent and have proven yourself as someone who can be trusted. Organizers and organizations (and even companies) can become more trustworthy by being transparent and responsible. And by being responsive to current events without trying to capitalize on them. Most importantly, they can become more trustworthy by being responsive to critique and holding themselves accountable.

**Rasheed: There's been a surge of censorship, surveillance, and exploitation not only on Instagram, but on the Internet in general. How have you seen this combatted and what does your digital utopia look like?**

**Nina:** I've seen a lot. Maybe because I have a lot of family who participated in the social movements of the 1960s and '70s and they're very careful and have a lot to say about surveillance. So I've always been super careful. I've always been very nervous about that and then I see on Instagram a lot of pages are shadow-banned, and then their work isn't circulated and people don't get to see it. It doesn't pop up in their timeline and stories and things like that. I know it's real and I know that people are using surveillance to arrest people, to find out where they are when people check into places, or list where they are. I feel very protective of you at this point, so I want to make sure you're being as careful as possible and not putting yourself in harm's way unnecessarily. But the second thing is, surveillance is real and it's being used. I think part of it is that you just have to be mindful of sharing the truth and being liberatory in ways that are not putting you in danger.

**Stephanie:** Yeah. I'm not as careful or mindful as Nina is but I am, in my own ways. You know, when I post my niblings or family, I don't ever post their names. I feel like little things like that, on Twitter especially, are super important. I have a couple of family members that use Twitter and I don't tag them. I have been doxed, and that was unnerving. My utopia is a place where I can share freely, have that public, and not worry about it.

**Rasheed: Cool. So, we talked about this a little earlier when we were talking about mutual aid. In the last year, we've seen a rise in mutual aid projects and groups. Why would you say that mutual aid is important?**

**Stephanie:** I think for all the reasons that we talked about. The system ain't it. The system ain't going to do it. I've also seen a lot of people comment about how mutual aid is what we call it at this moment, but mutual aid is what our folks have always done. You'll hear Indigenous folx talk about slaughtering an animal and going to the families that can't—or don't have somebody who can—go out and make sure they have enough meat to eat. Or our big mama making sure that the other kids on the block have food or intentionally placing dinner on the table while your friends are over because you know they don't have food at home. That's what we've always done. We frame it as mutual aid now, and I think that's useful, but I think it's also important to recognize that it's a tradition.

**Nina:** I can't add anything else to that. It is who we are to take care of each other.

**Rasheed: What do you see for the future of digital organizing? How do you see social media continuing to impact and drive our movements?**

**Stephanie:** Honestly, I don't know. I know that Black folks are adaptive people. We will continue to use social media to build movements, community, and joy. And, as social media continues to shift to suit capitalism, we will continue to subvert it to suit our needs. The world can never steal our ability to innovate. We will always have an answer.

**Rasheed: What are three words that you use to would describe the** *Phreedom Jawn* **page to someone else?**

**Stephanie:** Joyful. Honest. Timely.

**Nina:** Black. Free. Rasheed.

**Rasheed: I really just thank y'all for caring. Overall, just caring about everything and caring about me, caring about the well-being of other folx and just being vulnerable right now in this moment.**

**Stephanie:** I just want to say thank you again. Thank you for being for us. Meaning all Black folks. Thank you for joy. Thank you for the balance of it. Thank you for knowing that that's part of it. That's it.

**Nina:** We love you.

# Students Show Up: The Formation of the Philadelphia Black Students Alliance (PBSA)

Philadelphia Black Students Alliance

The Philadelphia Black Students Alliance (PBSA) was formed in July 2020 to ensure that Black students matter in all of our schools. Founded by Sheyla Street—a former student of the Masterman School[1]—after several racial incidents and at the behest of students, the PBSA made a series of demands for the proper treatment and support of Black students across the Philadelphia school system. What follows are the stories of the student organizers, how the PBSA formed, and what it means to hold Black students' experiences and educations as indispensable at a time when Black lives everywhere are being threatened, marginalized, and cut short.

## Sheyla Street's story

In May 2020, I met Ms. Tamara Anderson from the Racial Justice Organizing Committee through Ms. Lorene Cary and Mr. Thomas Quinn because of my work with "Vote That Jawn." My preparation for a citywide voter registration drive with Ms. Tamara introduced me to what I had been searching for my whole high school career. Less than a month later, in the beginning of June 2020, Ms. Tamara invited me

---

1. The Julia Reynolds Masterman Laboratory and Demonstration School is a middle and secondary school located in Philadelphia. It is a magnet school, located in the Spring Garden neighborhood. It is ranked second in Pennsylvania and 18th in the nation.

to attend a town hall for students about the Uprising put on by the Coalition for Transforming Trauma and Violence.[2]

I won't lie, I was a little nervous. I did not know what to expect. Although there were shootings on my block growing up and I'd lost a few neighbors due to gun violence, I still did not feel that my background qualified me to be on a call about transforming trauma and violence. This violence, ironically, did not feel close enough to me. That is the nature of Philly. Because I had not lost my brother or a close friend, I thought of my experience as normal. But of course, hearing gunshots on your block and seeing blood on the street is not normal.

During this town hall, I ended up meeting and working with Ms. Hannah Gann, who is now a part of the Philly Black Students Alliance as a nonstudent representative. Not only did I end up working with Ms. Gann, but I also got other Black students at Central High School—who are now also part of the PBSA—to join in the online event "Philly Youth Speak Out: Transforming Trauma and Violence in School."

This speak-out was the first time I had spoken outside of school about my experiences as a Black student at Masterman, a middle and secondary magnet school in Spring Garden. Although I spent hours after school working on Masterman's diversity committee, testifying, and recounting memories of students referring to my people as monkeys and "niggers," I had never gone on the record about my experience in front of people who were not even involved.

Prior to the speak-out, I always looked at my speaking out as complaining. Whether it was a white teacher who asked me why I isolated myself while I sat in a room full of white kids who used the N-word and asked me when I would get over slavery, or if it was this same white male teacher who discouraged me from attempting the harder math problems, I did not think my experiences deserved to be heard so I hesitated to speak out about it outside of the school.

I transferred from Masterman to escape its pervasive racism and one-dimensional perceptions of my character. Leaving Masterman was a sacrifice, but I believe it was well worth it. My successful transfer to

---

2. See Philly Youth Speak Out: Transforming Trauma & Violence in School, July 8, 2020, https://www.pacesconnection.com/g/philadelphia-aces-connection/event/philly-youth-speak-out-transforming-trauma-and-violence-in-school.

Central gave me confidence. Without leaving Masterman, I'm not sure if I would have met Ms. Gann and the rest of the Racial Justice Organizing Committee, who uplifted my voice and my story. After I spoke out on July 2, they wanted to hear more and invited me to speak on July 12.

When TeachKizzyTeach, also known as Ms. Keziah Ridgeway, spoke at the Educators and Students for Black Lives March on July 12, 2020, I was inspired. Inspired to speak out, to get involved, and to organize. On the same day, when I saw Dr. Akbar back at her alma mater, Masterman, standing with Black students, I felt motivated to organize for the people coming after me. When Ms. Wesley took on becoming Central High School's Director of Equity and Inclusion in October 2020, before we could secure a fully released position for her, I knew I could balance being an organizer, student, and athlete. Our nonstudent representatives, all of whom are Black women, exemplify what we strive to be and help us stay grounded as a group in the work. When we begin to get lost in our organizing and forget that we originally came together to be free, they remind us through their words and actions.

When I got the bullhorn and spoke on the mic at the Philly Educators and Students March for Black Lives, I did not feel nervous, but empowered. The supportive responses from the young crowd kept me going. Every time I spoke louder, people clapped more. So I released and let out the pent-up memories and opinions of being a Black student in a Philadelphia magnet school. Then I walked from 440 N. Broad Street back to my old school (Masterman) and watched other Black students experience this healing. They stood on those steps and spoke their truth. The beauty of the march that took place on July 12 is that we had demands to back up our testimonies.

A week after the July 12 march, I set up a Google Meet and invited all the people I was inspired by: Brandon Archer, Tatyana Roldan, Youma Diabira, Madison Tyler, Kayla Gibson, Ms. Keziah Ridgeway, Dr. Ginneh Akbar. We talked, reflected, and knew that we needed to stick together. The demands of the Racial Justice Organizing Committee, Black Students at Central, and Masterman's Alumni for Change Charter were the catalyst for getting the PBSA started. We realized we were doing similar work and would be more effective together.

### Youma Diabira's story

I grew up with five siblings in my house, and for as long as I can remember, I've had to advocate for myself. Whether it was to get the only pink popsicle in the freezer or the bunk bed I wanted. Growing up in the Philadelphia school district, I've had to advocate for safe environments for me to learn in as well. I went from fighting over frozen popsicles to fighting against racial injustice.

I am now a senior at Central High School. I first attended Masterman but I left due to the lack of Black students and teachers in the building. I had little to no support as a Black student at Masterman. I remember being a member of the "On the Town" cast in my eighth-grade year. After getting into a disagreement with a white cast member, she went and told her mom, who was a volunteer at the time, about her dislike for me. Her mother replied, "You don't have to worry about her for long. People like her don't get into high school." That was my final year at Masterman.

Upon transferring to Central, I was thrilled at the vast diversity of the student body. It had been so long since I had been in a school that had more than ten Black kids. I immediately joined Central's African American Student Union (AASU) and at the end of my first year, I was elected its Vice President. As the seniors who nurtured me into this position left, I realized how the Black population was deteriorating. My first year on the board we were faced with every obstacle. First, we had to fight to hold our annual Black History Month showcase. Shortly after winning that fight, we lost our International Day hallway decoration spot to the Recycling Club. Yes, you read that right. Seeing the racism that was inflicted by the administration gave me a new lens to view Central High School. Instead of it being that huge melting pot of cultures and identities, it quickly turned into every other anti-Black institution. My junior year, I was promoted to AASU's President. We began fighting racism within our school following several instances of students and teachers targeting Black students in the building. Unfortunately, COVID-19 hit the world pretty hard around March and resulted in schools being closed indefinitely. After spending hours in meetings discussing how we can change our school climate, everything just stopped. Jobs closed, schools stopped, but racism didn't.

On February 23, Ahmaud Arbery was murdered by racist residents in Georgia. On March 13, Breonna Taylor was murdered in her bedroom by police. On May 25, George Floyd was murdered by police. This sparked a revolution. Protests, riots, and petitions. It allowed me, as a Black female student in Philadelphia, to understand the result of racist behaviors and attitudes that have continued to persist and go unaddressed. It allowed me to see the impact of racist children and racist adults. I decided we had to do more. I decided that I had to do more.

My first virtual summer turned out to be my busiest. After meeting with other Black students at Central who shared the same sentiments, we decided we needed to take action. After several Zoom calls and much planning, we created a "10-Point Plan" for the eradication of anti-Blackness within Central High School.[3] After holding a town hall to explain our work to faculty, administration, and alumni, the support was indescribable. Immediately after, we began working with the administration to implement our demands within the school.

I was able to speak at the Educators and Students for Black Lives March about the detrimental effects of not having Black teachers, not learning Black history, and not reading Black literature. As students, our voices matter. They need to be heard. We deserve more as Black students in our schools. Unfortunately, this is not just a district issue, but a national issue too. We have to start somewhere. This is where a huge part of my collaboration began. I knew Sheyla Street and Brandon Archer, as I went to Masterman with them, but I was able to meet other students from other Philadelphia high schools who were having the same battles. I met Aniyah Harris and Shamiyah Boozer from Carver Engineering and Science as well as Tatyana Roldan from Northeast High School. This march was our moment. We were six students who knew we had to do more and that more was possible together. And now we have the Philly Black Students Alliance that represents Central High School, Masterman, Carver Engineering and Science, Northeast, Roxborough High, Palumbo High, Science Leadership Academy, and more. Who knew fighting for that pink popsicle would prepare me to help lead an entire movement? I got my pink popsicle. I'm working with these amazing leaders to get justice next.

---

3. To review Philly Black Students Alliance's "10-Point Plan," see Appendix.

### Mariame Sissoko's story

The beginning of my journey with PBSA started at the end of my tenure as a student in the school district. It was the middle of May 2020. I was a senior at Central during the beginning of a global pandemic and racial justice protests that reverberated across the world. As a Black student attending Central, I had dealt with one too many instances of racial aggression and inequity, and like so many, George Floyd's murder was a tipping point. Initially, a teacher by the name of Nicholas Palazzolo contacted Black student leaders at Central who in the past had pushed Central to make necessary changes to become antiracist. This was my first time meeting Youma Diabira and Sheyla Street, two people who would become instrumental in creating the Philadelphia Black Students Alliance. Together, the day before my graduation, we hosted a speak-out where Black Central students and alumni shared personal stories of racism they've endured while attending one of the top schools in the city. From the collective experiences of Black students, we crafted and presented ten demands Central needed to follow to improve Black student life. What we didn't know was that Black students at Masterman, another one of Philly's top magnet schools, were doing the exact same thing. This was the kernel that would become PBSA. Black students, not just at magnet schools, but across the city collectively screaming out "we've had enough!"

I spent the following summer before entering college attending protests, meetings, and speak-outs alongside Youma and Sheyla. I grew as a speaker and advocate. I realized no one would speak up for Black students but Black students, and if I wanted change for people who looked like me then I would have to be on the front lines. Through all this, Youma, Sheyla, and I worked with Elizabeth Wesley, the first-ever appointed Director of Equity and Inclusion at Central per Black student demands. We met Keziah Ridgeway, a teacher at Northeast High School; Brandon Archer, one of the creators of PBSA from Masterman and an alliance chairperson; and finally, Tatyana Roldan, another alliance chairperson from Northeast High School.

It became clear to us that the issues we faced were not localized in our individual schools but were problems spanning the entire school district. PBSA was born from the idea we were better speaking as one collective voice rather than multiple, individual schools working for our own gain. However, PBSA is more than the trauma Black students endure. It is bonding over our collective joy. Brandon, Sheyla, Youma, and Tatyana have turned a group based in trauma to one that celebrates Blackness and its beauty. From Black student hangouts to the Juneteenth celebration, PBSA is a space for Black Philly students to revel in our accomplishments while pushing our district to do better by us. Although I've moved on to Barnard College, I am proud to say I've played a small part in leaving the School District of Philadelphia a better place for Black students than when I entered.

**What the PBSA would tell other Black students about organizing**

Black students should know that unity is key when organizing. When students come together in support of something, everyone is forced to listen. Our energy and ability to reimagine are what prompt change. Change is uncomfortable but necessary. So when we collaborate, some people get nervous. However Black students should know that Black teachers like Ms. Wesley, Ms. Ridgeway, and Ms. Gann have their backs when others are ready to attack.

As organizers, it is our job to set certain standards for campaigns, events, and collaborations. Keeping the PBSA up to par while also balancing school and other activities has not been easy. Whether it is our partnerships, outreach, social media, or just basic communication to general members, we split tasks among ourselves to make it more manageable. While Shamiyah creates informational and motivational graphics for our Instagram to attract people to our organization, Youma, our outreach coordinator, is in charge of reaching out to potential members. Our chairpersons (Brandon, Sheyla, and Tatyana) send out emails, set up meetings, panels, and collaborations. We have event coordinators, Aniyah and Shamiyah; a secretary, Makayla, who makes sure all of our re-imaginative ideas are recorded; and a treasurer, Rebecca, who is in charge of collecting funds. Together we make up the core group of the Philly Black Students Alliance. We are in charge of the PBSA operations, but what makes our group is our general membership of Black students who come from various schools around the city and demonstrate the diversity, depth, and beauty of Black people.

# I Know You Are Doing Your Best: Prayer for Philadelphia

Charlyn Griffith

At the beginning of the coronavirus pandemic, my family found itself in a peculiar situation. Providing free produce to about twenty families weekly, hosting no-cost curated brunch events, and then suddenly houseless. In a critical moment, we tapped into our pastoral ancestors and spirit guides, including the Leni Lenape that, too, were once displaced from this land.

We made an extraordinary pivot. We marooned to the desert. Alongside the Chemehuevi land of the Mojave, 2,587 miles away from Philadelphia, I introduced my wife to sacred, gratifying accountability and she introduced me to intoxicating joy. For forty days and nights, we cast spells and made rituals in Mama Octavia E. Butler's California.

At the end of this auspicious season of upheaval, we bought, with seed money from our beloved community, a place that is both seed and fruit, nourishment and preparation. We thought we were being forced to build a home in chaos, but ten trips across the country in fourteen months we built a homestead oasis. While the pandemic demanded cautious contact, we provided the distance from Philadelphia and

A prayer and promise
                             for journey

('specially when you is ti-RED.
Because sometimes you pull a beloved closer,
even though you are also thinking GTFOHWTS)

I KNOW YOU ARE DOING YOUR BEST.
  • loving the unloved parts of your communities

- repairing that which you did not break
- giving generously of what some tried to take

thank you

Me and the beautiful ppl stolen to San Domingue which became Ayiti, from where so many Black Philadelphians came—conjured sweetness for your living now.

In the pages and words, in the flask I am holding rhum in for you when I meet you on the street. We are holding ritual for you already.

[Join us particularly with a rum drink or a dessert,
something chocolate even,
because cacao
& sugarcane are
OUR ancestors
and they too
built this city]

I love you.

My mother loves you.

She (from Trinidad & Tobago) say, "Take limes, milk, Florida Water, salt, and warm water in a bowl; say your prayers, say your name, and wash. Ask yourself forgiveness, ask yourself for help, say out loud what you want as you bathe. Let the air dry you. Rub yourself with olive oil and continue to pray for yourself, your family. Say the names out loud."

I say, "Dearest Parent, Spouse, Sibling & Friend God, Universe, angels, ancestors, saints, Orishas, Loa thank you. Thank you for the person reading these words right now. Thank you for giving breath and blood to their potential. Thank you for bringing us to this convergence for a collective experience of lives well lived. Thank you for focusing their energy today and where they will pivot to as they travel through time, finding many tomorrows. I ask on my own and their behalf that you all conspire to make the path easier. Please clear our senses, make them finely tuned to our missions. Make the calling a song that we joyfully bring our noise to. Please, consistently place coinciding events that show us our perfection, near us. Please let these words, which be the meditation of my heart, fill the reader and all those around them with hope and knowingness. Please let this passage be promise."

My chest heaves as the heart given to me
leaps
for
you.

Hold your hands
            if you are able
                        and imagine we
                                    walking
together.

# Navigating Collective Grief: How Organizers Wrestle with Persistent Loss

Cassie Owens

They were often honored in silence. The pandemic restricted memorials to small gatherings that often didn't feel much like funerals at all. In their place were quick services where, at times, only mere handfuls of people could appear without knowing if their loved ones were safe to touch. Memorials where mourners who'd come to view could be told there was no re-entry, where an internment might last only eight minutes, where a howl from the pews could be muted over Zoom for the majority of the bereaved listening. The dead were still remembered all the same. In balloon releases, on social media, in thoughts held but not spoken, the memories of the ones lost have always been present.

But are Black people free to remember our dead the way that we knew them in life? According to Johnny Silvercloud, editor-in-chief of *AfroSapiophile*, an online hub for Black writing and photography, Black people lack freedom of memory and are often memory-policed for referencing atrocities of the past that very much live in the present. Reading Silvercloud's essay on six freedoms Black people are denied under white supremacy—memory being one of them—last May, Kevin Carter, clinical director at the Uplift Center for Grieving Children, adapted Silvercloud's theory for his work. For Carter, freedom of memory would be "to remember things from your own perspective and also have access to a historical record that affirms actually who you are and what you're about," he explained.

Carter wonders if the family of Walter Wallace Jr. has the space to remember him on their own terms. Does the family of Dominique "Rem'mie" Fells have that space? Does the MOVE Organization have that freedom for Tree Africa, Delisha Africa, and the other family members they've lost? When George Floyd, Breonna Taylor, and Ma'Khia Bryant are vilified or turned into mascots, do their loved ones have freedom of memory?

When loved ones pass away, media depictions may misrepresent them, if there's any coverage at all, explained Tori Gillis. Gillis is a community advocate who devotes much of her efforts to marginalized youth, including those from Black and queer communities and young people experiencing housing insecurity. She said that without memory, the work would be pointless. "[The coverage] forces us to keep that person in the positive light that we remember," Gillis said. "Remembering is important because you don't want to let the legacy of a person be forgotten. Even if the memory hurts," she added. "You don't want what they've been through with the experience and what you felt from that experience to be lost because it means you can't truly tell a person about their legacy, you can't tell them what they've been through. And then you also can't tell them how to get through it."

The challenges of the last year have been heavy, explained Gillis. These days, Gillis can see signs of progress, but explains that the grief is still a lot to carry. She's lost people in her community who she'd *just* seen, colleagues, and a dear, dear friend who was like a brother. When she's needed to cry, she's allowed herself to. When she's needed some time to herself, she's taken it. Her commitment has stayed, but she now sees the past in a different light.

"I feel like this year just kind of gave me a glimpse into what people doing the [movement] work have had to go through in history, in Black history," Gillis said. "And in the civil rights movement and the Stonewall movements. [Those organizers] lost lots and lots of people; they've hit some really high highs and some devastating lows. [The last year] hasn't changed my outlook; it just gave me a better understanding and a better appreciation for what was done for us prior to now."

Gillis is not alone. In interview after interview, organizers and advocates explained that in one way or another, they were looking back as they charted a way forward through the pain. To help manage their grief and to learn from the past, Saudia Durrant, a racial justice organizer at the Abolitionist Law Center who worked closely with the Philadelphia Student Union in 2020, has been reading more. Delving into books—like bell hooks' *All About Love*, Audre Lorde's *Sister Outsider*, Irik Robinson's *Black Seed*, and Mumia Abu-Jamal's *We Want Freedom*—challenged her attachment to social media and devices in a good way, she explained, and pushed her to look for deeper connections.

Durrant has also had to heal from different forms of grief. Before the pandemic, in the span of a few years in the 2010s, she lost several relatives, among them her father, grandmother, and aunt. This past December, she had to deal with the grief she felt while sick from COVID-19. How Black people experience loss, Durrant said, but also the conditions of those losses, deeply informs her work. "Something that's been really helpful for me in my organizing and in my personal life is to see death and the deaths that have happened as reason to move with as much intention and power as possible," said Durrant.

Some have always known, others have gained more language during the consciousness raising of the last year: COVID-19 is another crisis that disproportionately impacts Black people and leads to premature and preventable deaths. Like murders by police, gun violence, maternal death, HIV, asthma, diabetes, lethal intimate partner violence, hate crimes across the board, and so on.

Christina Sharpe, a Delaware County native and expert of Black studies and visual culture, connects the "always possible deaths" of Black people to the anti-Black climate of everyday society, shrouded in the afterlife of slavery. In her book *In the Wake*, she points to this sentiment expressed by Frantz Fanon in *The Wretched of the Earth*: "We revolt simply because, for many reasons, we can no longer breathe." Just as tracing the prevalence of these conditions draws a line that is inextricable from structural racism and racial enclosure, and just as Black people have experienced higher mortality rates than their white counterparts for generations, there is a longstanding relationship between Black resistance movements, memorial, and work for survival.

Social epidemiologist Sharon Jones-Eversley researches how Black Americans experience chronic death exposure and the grief pipeline.[1] With death exposure, explains Jones-Eversley, "people start realizing

---

1. Sharon D. Jones-Eversley and Johnny Rice II, "A call for epidemiology and thanatology to address the dying, death, and grief pipeline among Blacks in the United States," *Death Studies*, February 2020, https://www.tandfonline.com/doi/abs/10.1080/07481187.2020.1721618?journalCode=udst20.

this is so much pain, on top of racism, on top of so many other things. And then we're hit with COVID-19. For me, it's like, we're fighting for the living. And those who are yet to come. There's a sense of urgency and relevance."

Kempis "Ghani" Songster, a founding member of the Coalition to Abolish Death by Incarceration and Right to Redemption (R2R), was working with Amistad Law Project,[2] where for some months they held community conversations on Zoom. It was a space where everyone had been managing the tolls of mass incarceration and the pandemic. Those talks over Zoom served as one type of medicine, but Songster, who now works as a restorative justice diversion program manager at the Youth Art Self-Empowerment Project, would need other medicines too. "I came out [of prison in 2017] with a strong sense of survivor's guilt, you know, kind of like, the only one to survive in a car accident full of people," he explained. "So, that's why I steep myself in the movement, hoping that something that I could do can help open the door for those people to come home as well, and live out the rest of their lives with dignity and surrounded by their family and the people who love them.

"And so, hearing that, you know, they passing away one by one because of the virus behind the walls, and because of the institutions, because of the prison system's response to the virus—which is responding to it not in a public health way, but in a punitive way, locking people down—it's kind made me feel like, *yeah, damn, you failed kinda.*" To deal with that feeling, he meditates every day. He wonders if people know how deep organizers have had to dig to keep going. He wonders, after this difficult era passes, "Will we still be human? Will we still be who our ancestors wanted us to be?"

One of the medicines that's kept him going has been watching his toddler develop and grow. Like Gillis, he's been a student of history, with an eye toward diasporic Maroon communities. The last year sent Songster, who had an asymptomatic case of COVID-19, back to healing traditions his family used in Trinidad and Tobago. Speaking of the remedies his family revived, Songster said, "We were digging in the cultural crates."

---

2. Amistad Law Project is a public interest law firm and organizing project, founded in October 2014, working to end mass incarceration in Pennsylvania and fighting to get our communities the resources they need to thrive.

"Your gingers, your garlics, your cinnamon bark, your star anise, your peppers," he continued. "Your vinegars and different plants, your sages, your bay leaves, you know. Putting it all together and making broth, watching videos of other herbalists and healers from the Islands. Not saying that we believed we could come up with some kind of miracle remedies or cures and stuff, but just trying to think of anything we could do that our ancestors passed down to us, that nature gave us, to fortify ourselves. We were sharing that over the phone, over videos."

Sadly, for many Black Philadelphians, grief has never been a stranger. And grief can turn up anytime, unannounced, to amplify the pain of a loss you still feel, then remind you of the losses you felt before.

Carter explained that grief can manifest in ways other than sadness: as headaches, for example, or neck pain, or stomach discomfort, or insomnia, or rage. Carter described our society as not only death-denying but also grief-denying, yet in these times, there's too much grief to ignore. "You know you don't know when you're going back to your job, you don't know whether your child's going to school, you don't know how they're going to school," Carter said. "So a lot of these things that we thought were basic elements of our society are now under the rubric of grief and loss."

Along with freedom of memory, Carter noted that Black people don't always have access to freedom of expression with grief or freedom to defend ourselves [from white supremacy and state-sanctioned violence]. Grief, as Carter explained, can show up in your body. It can be energy draining. But at the same time, Carter said, grief can be a motivator. Expressions of grief can be good for a person, he continued, citing art as an example. He describes it as a challenge, but one that's "well worth taking." Working with his clients at the Uplift Center for Grieving Children, Carter doesn't deny their lived experiences or realities, and focuses on how to support them. He checks in about what's working for them and may ask: "What are some of the natural things that you're already doing to settle your body? Are you writing? Are you walking? Can you exercise? Can you still call your friends? Can you still connect with your family?"

Maintaining connection to people who've died, with the support of community, is something that Carter considers "culturally laden." "I think the work for us moving forward is when people are living, how do we stay connected, then when people die, how do we help people stay connected to them in ways that they feel like they want and need?" Carter continues, "I think young people are very much attuned to that—that connection is long existing, and that connection is forever. I think adults may be the ones who sanction those endings and them [kids] needing to move on."

The last year has shown Durrant that it falls to her and other organizers to find meaning in all they do. "There's been this thing culturally of like, you know, YOLO [You Only Live Once]," Durrant said. "Like thinking recklessly or just doing whatever we want, whatever feels immediately gratifying. And this year has definitely forced me— through experiencing a lot of deaths—to disrupt or to challenge that." Gillis has long worked through her grief. For her, the bottom line is that the work goes on. The work of combatting violence against Black transwomen or raising awareness of how media coverage "minimizes what that loss really means," or the work of increasing visibility for the community, and so on, is all still there. She's working to see all those changes but is also hoping to see a change in care. "Being a little more empathetic to the people in the community because that one thing could stop parents from putting their kids out of their house, that stops homelessness, that stops underage sex work for these kids," she said. "If you have a little more compassion and understanding, then there'll be a little more protection for those people. I would like to see more love in general."

Grief, as Dr. Mari Morales-Williams explains, can also be a teacher. An educator and restorative justice facilitator, they recall a day working at the North Philadelphia farm Urban Creators not too long after starting there. They were grieving the job they'd left at a school community they cared for deeply. It was a Friday in May, the gray cloudy sky reminded them of "an opal without the iridescent tinge to it." They were weeding a potato patch when the "yes, healing, but also backbreaking" experience of tending the land made them feel how sorely they could use a massage. And in that moment, that type of touch felt out of grasp. "I just sort of like fell back onto the earth and started to roll around and get this mini-massage, and I got emotional," recalled Morales-Williams, who now works as a healing justice advocate at the abolitionist lobbying group Straight Ahead! They were releasing like they hoped to, but it was also a reminder of ancestral knowledge, of having a spiritual connection with the land.

"It was a deep dropping in. I think it was Zora Neale Hurston who talked about that: there's a sense of words within us, but underneath that place of words is a place of wordlessness," they said. "I think that's the place where ancestral wisdom is also housed. . . . That interconnectedness with accepting and surrendering to a bit of mystery, but also feeling sort of grounded in this certainty of self as you move."

Janine Africa, Janet Africa, and Ramona Africa, like many activists, have been organizing at home. They have been pushing for Mumia Abu-Jamal's release, along with other activists who share profound concern that Abu-Jamal is experiencing deathly levels of medical neglect. (According to the *Philadelphia Tribune*, Abu-Jamal, who had already been ailing from multiple medical conditions, lost thirty pounds after contracting COVID-19 in prison.)[3] Staying in the struggle despite isolation hasn't felt new to Janet Africa. She thinks back to how they'd work over the phone when she was incarcerated. "It was always a constant communication. And because our belief is so strong, we didn't feel like we was imprisoned and locked away from everything, because we were still involved, and people outside were involving us. So, it just kept on going," Janet Africa said. "And when that COVID hit real hard, and people couldn't go anywhere, it was so familiar to us that it didn't hinder us at all."

Their norm for many years has been to not let grief hinder them either. The devastations they experienced—in the 1978 siege, 1985 bombing, and during decades of incarceration for nine of the Africas—have deepened their resolve. Before it was common to see organizers prioritizing connecting with the land, and formerly apolitical demonstrators filling crowds at mass protests, or national media applying a more critical lens to police violence, the MOVE Organization had been familiar with grief. Observing how attitudes have shifted around police brutality, Janine Africa thinks people are starting to understand what they, at the MOVE Organization, have long known:

---

3. Michael D'Onofrio, "Mumia Abu-Jamal loses 30 pounds while recovering from COVID-19," *Philadelphia Tribune*, March 8, 2021, https://www.phillytrib.com/news/local_news/mumia-abu-jamal-loses-30-pounds-while-recovering-from-covid-19/article_c5da1e74-7639-5161-8558-57a7d68a2dd8.html.

"Because of the Panthers, MOVE, the things that we experienced at the hands of this government—people really didn't want to get involved," she said. "They felt like, 'Well, y'all must be doing something wrong. If we be quiet and follow the laws, that won't happen to us. And I don't believe that the police did this to you' and on and on and on...."

Janine Africa thinks what it took for people to see otherwise is really a shame. But she's glad that the tone has shifted, that people still aren't insisting: "'I'm not involved, my child will be safe, I'll be safe.'" She explains, "Because now they're sitting there in their living rooms, watching their children be shot down on TV, it's no longer, 'well, if y'all wouldn't mess with the police, the police wouldn't mess with you.'"

The system, John Africa taught them, is murderous and is not going to stop. That's why they've always stood up for themselves. For Ramona Africa and her family, resigning from liberation work due to their grief is not an option. The work towards liberation, for her and for so many, remains connected to how she honors the people she's lost. "What keeps me going is that I will not let what happened to our family be in vain," Ramona Africa said. "Because our family fought this system, including our children, and never gave in. So how can I give in? I can't. I have to keep on fighting for my family."

Cassie Owens has written stories about the Paul Robeson House & Museum for *The Philadelphia Inquirer* in 2020. Because of this, she declined compensation for ethical reasons. Per her request, the How We Stay Free editors donated the honorarium for Owens' work to Dignity Housing. Dignity Housing's mission is to break the cycle of homelessness and poverty that confronts low-income families and individuals in Philadelphia. They work to fulfill their mission through the provision of transitional and long-term housing in combination with supportive services that create opportunities and promote self-sufficiency. Learn more about them at https://www.dignityhousing.org.

# Building a Legacy of Liberation in Black Families

Jared Michael Lowe

I was five years old when an almost all-white jury found three of the four Los Angeles policemen who savagely beat Rodney King "not guilty." It was 1992, and though I can barely remember graduating from kindergarten that summer, I vividly recall the verdict's aftermath, the anger and anxieties of the Black elders around me, and the emotional toll that King's assault left on them for years to come. All those feelings resurfaced last year watching then seventeen-year-old Darnella Frazier's nearly ten-minute-long cellphone video of George Floyd's final moments in the hands of law enforcement.

It was a macabre déjà vu that brought me back to my five-year-old self watching the grainy black-and-white videotape of King's assault. Those memories returned in flashes: seeing my grandmother's pained expression upon hearing the verdict on the evening's news report—her brows furrowed and chestnut-colored eyes alit with a mélange of rage and concern, the news reports of storefronts ablaze in Los Angeles, the orange glow so bright I thought the devil would rise and take the city, the images of the US Army, Marines, and the National Guard descending upon the burning city with guns and tanks, and the way the grownups at the cookouts that summer screamed and shouted in rage from the verdict, their beer floating out the lips of their cans and bottles, followed by a hushed, awkward silence whenever my young cousins and I entered a room.

At the time, I couldn't make sense of what happened to King and why Los Angeles burned. My parents weren't forthcoming with information, nor did I ask. I was too afraid to even mutter a word around them as I didn't want to rile them. I understood the context clues. They'd change the topic when it would come up in conversations if I happened to be in the room or turn the channel on our television whenever there was a news report or update. I had an instinct that they didn't want to talk to me about it, nor would I have understood the gravity of what happened.

Though they didn't sit me down and tell me why King was assaulted, or the preeminent danger Black people face whenever police are involved, they showed it through their actions. It was in the way they tucked me in at night, reassuring me that no one was going to come after us while we slept. Or, in the stories that they read to me of Black heroes like Marcus Garvey, Harriet Tubman, W.E.B. DuBois, or Madame C.J. Walker; folks who eclipsed their obstacles to become leaders, entrepreneurs, and visionaries. And it was passively in their sayings over the years to "reach higher" and to "not let anyone, even a person who looks different from you, make you feel less than." Over the years, I came to understand it as their way of shielding me from the pervasiveness of racial violence for as long as they could, hoping that I could retain some insular form of happiness that Black children can only be ensured of in homes where they are safe and loved. And though I still never received the talk or longed for them to be open and honest with me about King's assault and the many instances of violence against Black people since then, I understand now how they cultivated liberation in our home.

"I get now that they wanted to protect us," my cousin, Alyssa, shares with me via Zoom. Like me, she witnessed King's assault as a child, and like me, her parents—my aunt and uncle—chose not to talk to her or her younger siblings about racialized violence against Black people. "Today, it's different. We had to sit down and talk to Avery [her son] about George Floyd because he came to us about him. He watched the video, heard the news, and talked about it in his classroom. It was on Nickelodeon and Sesame Street. It was everywhere. We chose to tell him."

Alyssa and I connect over Zoom periodically. Though the pandemic has left us physically distanced for over a year, we've found ourselves growing closer while apart. She lives in Cherry Hill, New Jersey, is married, has a seven-year-old son, Avery, and at the time of writing this essay, has another child on the way. She's a former middle school teacher who recently was promoted to administrator. During the Uprising, we talked fairly often about her role as both a Black mother and teacher in a primarily white, though rapidly diversifying, suburban enclave, communicating to her child and the students in her classroom about the occurring events. "With my students, I have to 'walk the line' because as a teacher, my role is to instruct, to state the facts, and help them process what is going on," Alyssa says. "Avery's my child, so I can be candid with him."

Avery is an intelligent, imaginative, and determined seven year old. Already he has his sights on becoming both an artist and engineer when he grows up. He's shown this to me many times, showing me whatever latest roller coaster built with his LEGOs or constructing plays with his action figurines. In many ways, he reminds me of myself at that age, creative and intuitive. Watching him over the years, I can't help but hope that he, like so many Black children of today, grows up with an assurance that we tell them the unvarnished truth about how the world sees us and how we see ourselves.

"We're trying to prepare him with the tools, even at this age, to handle himself accordingly," Alyssa says. "I want him to stand strong as a Black creative little boy and walk with his head held high. If obstacles come in the way because of what he looks like or who he is, I don't want him to fall or crumble." Last year, Alyssa and her husband, Artis, talked with Avery about George Floyd's death after watching an hour-long town hall special on Sesame Street and CNN. Sesame Street characters Big Bird, Elmo, Abby Cadabby, and Rosita, along with CNN journalists, answered questions submitted by families that addressed the complex topic of racism in America. The start of the town hall featured Elmo's dad, Louie, explaining to his son why people are protesting. "We watched it as a family, and then after we talked it over with him," Alyssa says. "We kept having that conversation throughout the year. We had to explain to him that there are good police officers and bad police officers like there are good and bad people in the world because his godfather is a cop, so that one episode of Sesame Street really opened the doors for us to have nuanced conversations with him about right and wrong, protest, police officers, and resilience."

During the summer, Alyssa, Artis, and Avery participated in a march in their township. The protest was small; no more than fifty people showed up, all families from various different backgrounds. Avery made a sign that read: "Enough is Enough! We need change!" Alyssa sees the protest as a "first step" in showing Avery to stand up for what he believes in. "He has to learn the truth—that's something that our parents wouldn't have done, but I need him to leave here protected. So, I can't hide the truth from him because I need him to come back home to us."

Similarly, last June, Dr. Anyabwile Aaron Love, a professor of History and Black Studies at Community College of Philadelphia, along with his partner and six-year-old son Coltrane, participated in an organized rally near the Philadelphia Museum of Art on the Parkway. It was a peaceful protest, one of several demonstrations that occurred due to George Floyd's death. Coltrane brought a sign that he made as he marched, finding other kids as he and his family went along. For Love, protesting is a form of resilience that he discovered in his youth, having attended rallies for the release of Mumia Abu-Jamal from prison and responding to the assault on King. Love believes having Coltrane participate in protests and demonstrations builds a culture of liberation, providing his son with the opportunity to see the world as it is freely, and be empowered to speak up for his community and others. "We're raising him with a political sense of what is going on in the world," says Love. "But we're not raising him to fight the war right now because he still needs to be a child. We're showing him ways he could in the future."

"You have to be honest with them," Margaret Day tells me over the phone. Day is the Associate Director of Emotional Support and a student counselor at Freire Charter School in Philadelphia. "For most kids, by fourth or fifth grade, they've pretty much figured out what they believe in terms of race, gender/sexual orientation, class/socioeconomic status, and ability. But kids ages four and five begin to understand differences at that age. They're beginning to think critically about actions and situations that affect them."

Day says that having difficult conversations around race, protest, and movement work may feel uncomfortable for some parents. "Some parents feel like they have to be right and always show strength in front of their children, and that's not always the case. Parents don't have to have all the answers figured out to discuss these pressing events or topics with their children. It's fine to admit that they are worried, scared, or concerned and that they have questions, too." By opening up to children and allowing for vulnerability, Day suggests, parents can foster a way for their children to connect with them, allowing them to see their parents as their whole selves and not these strong robotic beings who don't have feelings. "Although our children are young and unable to actively participate in our conversations, part of my husband and I's work and stance is to have these weighty conversations amongst ourselves, openly, and in the presence of our children," says Janay Garrett, Assistant Dean of Student Affairs at Yale University. "We don't hide or shield them from conversations, though we are mindful of what might be developmentally appropriate. We have to be able to connect with them and build community."

Garrett is earning her PhD at the University of Pennsylvania, where her research and work is around Black mothers, and by extension, Black families. She aims to elevate the experiences of Black mothers, center their development and humanity (beyond motherhood and reproduction), and advocate for the transformation of contexts under which Black women become mothers. In her practice and care of other mothers, she models her own—her children are often in class with her, giving lectures and talks with students while they are in the room. For her, building liberation within her family is a form of modeling. "We try to create a culture of liberation in our family through the ethic of love, so that means speaking about love explicitly, demonstrating it, and being ok with it. Sometimes, it looks like connecting our children to the traditions of their grandparents or great-grandparents. Other times, it looks like affirming them, every chance they get, to instill a sense of personal and cultural pride." Garrett says that this also means speaking about Black folks in affirming and loving ways and actively resisting engaging or indulging in conversations about canceling folks or respectability politics.

In framing movement work with her children, Garrett says they started with books, film, music, and other forms of media. "We started with children's books, *A is for Activist* and *Counting on Community.* We read it every single day, and I remember my daughter vividly learning the word "activist" as one of her earliest words and how she used to chant "p-p-power to the p-p-people!" Living in Philadelphia during the height of the protests, Garrett and her husband could not take to the streets and march with others as she was pregnant and her children, now two and four, were small. However, they would talk about what was happening in the city, especially when there were marches through town.

Instead of attending marches, they took their children to talks by local community organizers or activists and, when it was possible, exposed them to community spaces designed around mutual aid, collective care, and community arts. "It is important that we expose them to what this kind of work is so that one day we can hope that they participate and help others along the path towards liberation."

The next time I talked to Alyssa was the day that Derek Chauvin, the former police officer who was charged with the murder of George Floyd, was found guilty on all three counts: second-degree unintentional murder, third-degree murder, and second-degree manslaughter. The jurors had deliberated for more than ten hours and over two days before coming to their decision. Alyssa and I sat on our Zoom call, pondering whether justice was served in Chauvin's trial or was this a paltry measure of accountability. Chauvin's verdict cannot bring back George Floyd or eradicate state-sanctioned racialized violence and murder. Alyssa, also grappling with mixed emotions about the trial's outcome, understands that she's going to have to talk about justice to Avery. "It's something that I have to think about," Alyssa tells me after a brief pause. "Because I feel like justice wasn't served at all—nothing can bring back George Floyd, Breonna Taylor, Ahmaud Arbery, and so many others." Suddenly, Avery comes into camera view, smiles, and proudly shows me a new toy, an action figurine he recently received. Seeing his face light up as he describes the figurine and the level of detail, I once again see myself at his age, though less expressive and self-possessed. In him, I see what the future holds and how my cousin has already established a foundation where he is celebrated and liberated but, most importantly, loved.

After our call, Avery jets off to bathe and then to bed. It's 9 p.m., and Alyssa already knows that tomorrow morning her son will ask her what justice means and if justice was served after the murder of Floyd. She's wary and hesitant. "You got this. Look at the legacy that you are already forming with him. It's right there." I tell her, and she smiles, knowing that she will tell her son the truth as she has done with everything else.

# Untitled

Jasmine Combs

## I.

Outside I hear the sirens sing of death
Helicopters cackling low in the evening sky
like metal mosquitoes
A war cry from a masked face
And the sleeping boy
brushes a finger light against my forearm
calming me back into dream.

Of course I'd fall in love
while the world is burning.

And if it all truly is on fire
find me folded up in my lover's arms.
His laughter,
a peace pressed gently against my lips
melting into day.

## II.

And then the sky went dark.
Somewhere someone scalpels my mother open
And the thunder just keeps on rolling
And maybe
a rainbow is just another promise
God doesn't plan to keep.

They say, *in Islam*
*rain omens a blessing.*

I watch two fairy lovers flutter and dance
in the puddles
And cry
And pray
Even to my grandmother's God.

# Afterword: Protect Life

Christopher R. Rogers in conversation with Mike Africa Jr.

On the day of August 19, 2021, as the anthology approached its final revisions, editor Chris spoke with Mike Africa Jr. about what sustains him within Black liberation movements and the lessons that were revealed to him during Philadelphia's 2020 Black Uprising. A second-generation member of the MOVE Organization, Mike was born in a Philadelphia jail to his mother Debbie Africa and his father Mike Africa Sr., following a violent police raid on his parents' home. They were two members of the MOVE 9, arrested on false charges and unjustly sentenced to 100 years in prison.[1] At thirteen, Mike Africa Jr. began working to free his parents from prison. After over twenty-five years of struggle, and with the support of his family and attorney Brad Thomson, Mike successfully brought his parents home—along with several other members of the MOVE 9. Released separately months apart, Debbie Africa and Mike Africa Sr. were reunited at home in 2018. Continuing to organize for the freedom of political prisoners such as Mumia Abu-Jamal, Mike Africa Jr. remains a revolutionary.

**Christopher Rogers: Mike, what has sustained you within this work?**

**Mike Africa Jr.:** What really sustains me is I have a mission. I have a vision. When you're focused on the vision itself, you can align these

---

1. The MOVE 9 were innocent men and women who were sentenced to 30–100 years in prison following the August 8, 1978 massive police raid at their home in the Powelton Village neighborhood of Philadelphia. During the standoff, Philadelphia Police Officer James Ramp, who was street-level and facing the home, was killed by a single bullet that struck him on a downward angle. This evidence alone foreclosed the possibility for MOVE to have killed Ramp, since they were below street level, nestled in the basement of their home. Members of the MOVE 9 include: Debbie Sims Africa, Mike Davis Africa Sr., Janine Phillips Africa, Janet Holloway Africa, Merle Africa, Phil Africa, Delbert Orr Africa, Eddie Goodman Africa, and Chuck Sims Africa.

missions, these campaigns, in place. You work towards them. For a long time, my vision was to see my family out of prison. I had all these different small goals that built up to achieving the vision, which was seeing my parents free. Just like anything else, it's a job and you have to apply it to your life. For example, you may want to be a journalist. You got to take certain courses on journalism. You got to learn from other journalists. You got to speak to people that understand that world and use those experiences as steppingstones. You're going to get an opportunity to become a journalist, and that vision will be fulfilled. Yet, once that happens, you keep going. You begin to find the stories that journalists are supposed to tell, and then *that* comes to define who you are. That's what you do. That's the same way that I approached, working to free my parents, other members of the MOVE 9, and other political prisoners. You must have a vision. Having a vision is half of the work. Understanding your vision is half the battle. Maybe more than half.

What's the stage now for me? My parents are free. Now that they're out of those cages, we still must work to help support them. They're older people. The vision must change, evolve. The missions change. We work to find ways to help with their housing, and whatever else is required, to take care of them. Because the overall mission, the grand mission itself, is to protect life. That's the overall mission: Protect Life. You got to protect the life of that which is the closest to you, and the most important to you, and then allow that to extend out further and further.

I don't believe it's difficult to sustain a vision once you get clear about it. Once you're clear, it's not even really a choice. You believe in it. You envision yourself doing the work and you develop a commitment to it. Of course, the missions and getting certain jobs done might be hard sometime, yet you keep going. Because we need police-free streets. Because we need a true justice system as what we have now is an injustice system. Because these police running around town are innocent until proven guilty and meanwhile, we know it's the opposite for Black people. When you wholeheartedly know that you must make these changes, that's your vision. You know that you play a role in making that happen and you will never stop. Even when you get older and slow down and you realize you can't do it the same way you did when you were younger. You still find a way to consult, share your experiences, and spread your wisdom to others who have that energy. It never stops. It really never stops.

**Chris: We aspire for this collection to be around a while and reach audiences around the world with recollections of the 2020 Black Uprising in Philadelphia. Twenty to thirty years from now, what would you want people to remember about this moment?**

**Mike:** I believe the most important lesson that I learned from 2020 is never hide who you are. Never hide what your organization is about and what it's doing. Be transparent. Tell the story of your mission, and don't leave out the ups and downs. So many people are focusing on showing themselves shining, but they ain't showing themselves grinding. You can see the people on Instagram and Facebook. They show their muscles and their strength. They don't show you ten years before, when they had a gut hanging over their belt. How rare is it that we see activists at the roundtable? Those pictures aren't glorified the same but it's a crucial part of the work—when we are in those meetings, or when we are staying up late at night, when we are tired from looking at the computer screen. We must begin glorifying the inner struggles of the movement. We must begin glorifying and portraying the issues that we have going on within our interpersonal relationships that might not be so great. This is the work too. I want to make sure that we're transparent throughout because we never know how our harm, our misfortunes, our unfortunate situations stand to be the wisdom for all those coming behind us. We've got to allow people to see the work that it takes—the struggles, the falls, and all of it. This transparency, this vulnerability, is incredibly important, because within them are the moments that give us strength. They give us the experience and the wisdom to get up and keep on going to the next steps. Be transparent, don't hide nothing, and most of all, don't hurt nobody. That's it.

# Reflections: The Time Is Now

*"Many thousand gone . . ." but we, the living, are more firmly resolved: "No more driver's lash for me!" The dedicated lives of all who have fallen in our long uphill march shall be fulfilled, for truly "We shall overcome." The issue of freedom now for Negro Americans has become the main issue confronting this nation, and the peoples of the whole world are looking to see it finally resolved.*

*When I wrote in my book, Here I Stand, in 1958 that "the time is now," some people thought that perhaps my watch was fast (and maybe it was a little), but most of us seem to be running on the same time—now. The "power of Negro action," of which I then wrote, has changed from an idea to a reality that is manifesting itself throughout our land. The concept of mass militancy, of mass action, is no longer deemed "too radical" in Negro life. The idea that black Americans should see that the fight for a "Free World" begins at home—a shocking idea when expressed in Paris in 1949—no longer is challenged in our communities. The "hot summer" of struggle for equal rights has replaced the "cold war" abroad as the concern of our people . . . .*

*Yes, it is good to see all these transformations. It is heartening also to see that despite differences in program and personalities among Negro leadership, the concept of a united front of all forces and viewpoints is gaining ground.*

*There is more—much more—that needs to be done, of course, before we can reach our goals. But if we cannot as yet sing, "Thank God Almighty, we're free at last," we surely can all sing together: "Thank God Almighty, we're moving!"*

*PAUL ROBESON*
*New York*
*August 28, 1964*[1]

---

1.  Paul Robeson, *Here I Stand*, 2nd edition (Boston: Beacon Press, 1988), 120–121.

# Appendix

Demands and Vision:

# End the War on Black Philadelphia Now: 13 Demands outlined by the Black Philly Radical Collective

*We Want Freedom!*[1]

*End the War Against Black Philadelphians NOW!*
During this time of rebellion against police terrorism and state violence, we, the radical Black organizing community in Philadelphia, make the following immediately actionable demands upon the City of Philadelphia to abolish—by which we mean to eliminate permanently and holistically—the structures of policing and related state violence endangering our communities. These demands were written with the understanding that our more vulnerable family—our Black trans, disabled, and gender-oppressed community members—are especially targeted by the systems of oppressions expressed in our demands. We center the most vulnerable within our community in this document and in our work.

We will be in the streets demanding justice for the Black community until our demands are met.

## 1. We Demand an Authentic Defunding of the Police Budget

Since the Uprising began, the Philadelphia organizing community has made unequivocal demands for the City of Philadelphia to vote NO on a proposed increase to the police budget. In recent days, the city has responded to this public pressure and announced a reduction to the police budget by $33 million dollars. This supposed decrease in funding is simply a ploy by city officials to mislead the public. City Council has

---

1. Watch our June 27, 2020 press event announcing the Black Philly Radical Collective's "13 Demands" at https://youtu.be/SYJhQ_vHgbU.

merely moved the budget for crossing guards to another department of city government. This type of subterfuge is unacceptable. We demand an immediate and authentic reduction in the police budget by 20 percent. We want public funds to enrich our communities, not the police. We demand the originally proposed $14 million police budget increase be augmented by $11 million and go to the Philadelphia School District budget for the removal of environmental hazards from schools, namely, asbestos and lead paint, which is estimated to cost $25 million per year.

## 2. Immediately Cease the Criminalization of Black Resistance

We will not permit the Black community's legitimate struggle against white supremacy to be criminalized. Since the rebellion began, police have trapped and tear gassed protesters on I-676, they have unleashed rubber bullets and war munitions on 52nd Street in the heart of West Philadelphia, and they have brutalized protesters while arresting them as recently as Monday, June 22nd. The apologies of Mayor Kenney and Police Commissioner Outlaw about this treatment are not acceptable or accepted. We demand an end to the use of tear gas, grenades, assault rifles and surveillance in our neighborhoods and at the protests. We further demand that DA Larry Krasner drop all arrests and charges against community members and activists in relation to the rebellion and that no future detainment, arrests, or charges be made. We demand an independent and transparent investigation into the use of force against protesters as well as the extreme disparities in the use of force by police when confronting protests against police violence as opposed to white vigilantes in South Philadelphia and Fishtown.

## 3. Immediately and Permanently Remove All Symbols of State Violence

After decades of work by Philadelphia's Black organizers and community members, Mayor Kenney finally conceded to the demand to remove the statue of Frank Rizzo. Mayor Kenney has also agreed to remove the Christopher Columbus statue. We demand the immediate public destruction of these white supremacist symbols of hate, oppression, and violence so that they can never be erected elsewhere. The street sign honoring Wilson Goode is an equally flagrant symbol of state violence against Black Philadelphia, as former Mayor Goode presided over the bombing of our city and the murder of eleven members of the MOVE family, including five children in 1985. We demand that the street be reverted to its original name. We further demand legislation that removes all other existing monuments of state violence and ensures that no future symbols of state violence against Black, Indigenous, or Brown people be permitted in the City of Philadelphia.

*These first three demands require immediate action from the City of Philadelphia and are not negotiable. They represent immediate steps that the City must take to communicate its responsiveness to the demands of Black Philadelphians for justice for our communities.*

*We recognize the prison as an extension of police violence and demand the release of our incarcerated community members.*

### 4. Immediate Permanent Release of Mumia Abu-Jamal, Major Tillery, Arthur Cetawayo Johnson, Russell "Maroon" Shoatz, Omar Askia, Joseph "Jo-Jo" Bowen, and all Black Political Prisoners

The Philadelphia "justice system" that arrested and tried Mumia Abu-Jamal is the same racist and immoral system that dropped a bomb on eleven civilians including five children of the MOVE family thirty-five years ago. The fact that Mumia's trial was built on false evidence is without question and serves as proof of the history of Philadelphia police targeting those who speak out against state violence. In this period of COVID-19, we demand that Mumia, Major, Cetawayo, Maroon, Omar, Jo-Jo, and all Black political prisoners be immediately released. They are all seniors, members of a vulnerable population whose incarceration by any measure does not serve our communities or justice.

### 5. Immediate Release of All Vulnerable Individuals in Prison

Accelerate the release of the 1,800 individuals eligible under the reprieve order signed April 10, 2020, and expand this order so that all eligible individuals are released by the end of July, 2020. Include in your reprieve all individuals who are medically vulnerable regardless of their offense. Secretary Wetzel estimated that there are approximately 12,000 people currently incarcerated that would be considered "medically vulnerable." The order signed April 10th states: "Vulnerable inmates shall include inmates at risk based upon age, anyone with autoimmune disorders, who is pregnant, or who has serious chronic medical conditions like heart disease, diabetes, chronic respiratory disease, bone marrow or organ transplantation, severe obesity, kidney disease, liver disease, hepatitis, cancer, or any other medical condition that places them at higher risk for coronavirus, as defined by the Centers for Disease Control and Prevention." All trans and disabled inmates are also vulnerable and we demand that they be recognized as such and also released under the reprieve order.

*We demand a complete overhaul of the structures of police accountability.*

### 6. Swift Firing of Killer Cops and Community Response

We demand an end to superficial policies that assign desk duty and administrative leave for officer-involved shootings. If a police officer murders someone, they should be immediately and permanently fired and referred to counseling. The retirement funds of killer cops must be frozen during all parts of the legal process. If the officer is convicted, their pensions must be seized and transferred to the victim's families.

### 7. Abolish the Fraternal Order of Police (FOP) and the Police Advisory Committee (PAC)

The City government announced plans to create a Civilian Oversight Commission. Government officials have not been transparent about how this Commission will function or the amount of funding it will receive. We again demand that the PAC not be simply reformed, repackaged, and presented to the community as a progressive change. The Police Advisory Commission must be abolished and replaced with a fully funded Community Control Board provided from the budget of the Philadelphia police. The Board must have the exclusive power to hire and fire police officers. Board members must be elected through a transparent process that is created by individuals whose leadership is accepted by the community they will be representing. The members of this Board cannot be law enforcement or elected officials. The Board must also comprise community members most directly impacted by the system of policing. Their ultimate charge must be to remove all cops from our neighborhoods within five years. We also demand the FOP be dissolved immediately and police bargaining shifted into the municipal unions of the City of Philadelphia until the police are disbanded. The Fraternal Order of Police, its President, and agenda is more committed to defending police violence, terror, and mass incarceration than it is in protecting and serving Black Philadelphians. Through intimidation, bullying, and political intrigue it has set itself up as an unaccountable power bloc and political lobby that is a threat to our city's democracy.

*The Black community has the right to live safely without the threat of violence.*

## 8. End the Military Occupation of the Black Community

We demand the complete demilitarization of the Philadelphia police and the police occupation of Black communities. The Black community is consistently targeted by SWAT teams armed with military-grade equipment. We demand the city end any participation in the US Department of Defense's 1033 Program, and return any equipment acquired through it, and refuse any participation in Operation Relentless Pursuit, the Department of Justice's newest "war on crime" tactic. A local police force should not have the ability to engage with community members like enemy combatants.

## 9. Protection for Black Philadelphia

We acknowledge the severity of gun violence in our communities. Dismantling the structural violence of poverty, and not applying discriminatory gun laws, is the only way to create safe communities. Anti-Black violence, which is emboldened in the current white supremacist climate, is an ever-increasing threat to Black communities. Pockets of white vigilantes are currently roaming the city with guns, axes, and other deadly weapons in the wake of the rebellion. These extralegal white terrorist groups pose a significant risk to the Black community. We assert that Black Philadelphians have the ability to defend ourselves. We will no longer be criminalized for enjoying the 2nd Amendment rights that are permitted to all other Pennsylvanians. We demand that no current or future conceal/carry violations are registered as a felony in Philadelphia.

*Systems of carcerality and policing must be dismantled in all their forms.*

## 10. End All Carceral Systems

The destructive effect of mass incarceration on individuals, families, and communities extends beyond the prison walls. We demand an immediate end to the criminalization of race, poverty, mental health, ability, and immigration status through the multiple carceral systems that target Black Philadelphians. We demand the dismissal of warrants, cash bail, and the end to probation and parole systems that target our community members for prison retraumatization rather than provide support for individual and communal restoration. We demand the decriminalization of sex work. It is time to end the stigmatization and traumatization of sex workers through arrest and incarceration. We demand an end to the separation of Black families through the forcible removal of our children by the Department of Human Services. Children must be returned to willing parents and caregivers without ransoming their return with bureaucracy. We demand the City of Philadelphia live up to its promise as a Sanctuary City, immediately disband all Immigration and Customs Enforcement activities, and reunite individuals and families that have been separated because of ICE detainments in Philadelphia. We also demand that mental illness be decriminalized, and those with such disabilities be identified and provided the mental health care they require rather than assaulted by police and incarcerated.

## 11. Disband All Private Police Departments

Black Philadelphians are policed in virtually every area of our lives. Due to jurisdiction overlaps, a Philadelphian may be policed by Philadelphia Housing Authority police, transit police, university police departments, and city police simultaneously. We demand that the Philadelphia Police Department immediately end all Memorandums of Understanding with private police which allows access to JBAND frequency. We further demand that legislation be passed that mandates all public and private institutions, including educational institutions and transit and housing authorities, disband their police forces in the interest of public safety.

*Racist systems of oppression from slavery to the present must be addressed through economic justice.*

## 12. Fund Communities, Not Cops

We demand an immediate decrease in the Philadelphia Police Department's budget over five years until it is fully defunded. We demand these resources be diverted from policing to longstanding community-led organizations working to support returning citizens and build strategies that enable Black people to address their own conflicts and struggles in a manner that centers transformative justice and eliminates punitive systems of behavioral change. We demand the redistribution of these funds be decided by those who are directly impacted by the criminal legal system, including returning citizens, sex workers, our members of the disabled community, our LGBTQIA+ communities, and members of undocumented communities.

## 13. Economic Justice NOW!

We demand reparative economic justice for the aforementioned harms to Black communities. The government must repair the damage it has done. Current policies are designed to perpetuate racial and economic injustice against Black communities. We demand a participatory approach to public budgets that is under community control to ensure that resources are equitably distributed and meet the needs of Black communities which have been purposefully and systematically under-resourced. This is a critical step toward the realization of true reparative economic justice.

## SIGNATORIES

Philly for REAL Justice | Black Lives Matter Philly | The Black Alliance for Peace | Black and Brown Workers Cooperative | Abolitionist Law Center Philadelphia | Abolitionist Law Center Pittsburgh | Human Rights Coalition Philadelphia | Human Rights Coalition Pittsburgh | Mike Africa Jr. of MOVE | Mobilization for Mumia | International Family and Friends of Mumia Abu Jamal | Malcolm X Grassroots Movement

## Demands and Vision:

# Philadelphia Housing Action Demands[2]

*Disempower, disarm, and disband the Philadelphia Police Department and all private police departments.*

We lift up the demands of organizers from the Black Philly Radical Collective and our comrades at Philly for REAL Justice. You must meet their full demands.

1. The City must transfer ownership of Philadelphia Housing Authority (PHA), Philadelphia Redevelopment Authority (RDA), and Philadelphia Housing Development Corporation (PHDC) vacant property to a permanent community land trust for permanent low-income housing administered by local community control committees.

2. The City must put a moratorium against PHA, RDA, or PHDC buying, acquiring, obtaining, trading, auctioning, or selling off properties to private entities until all PHA waiting-list applicants have been housed and pending an independent study on the effects of mass sales and trade-offs on communities and community members.

3. The City must fire all cops and city or city-contracted workers that do not treat us with respect and dignity. The process must be public and transparent. You must stop cops from kicking people awake every morning.

4. The City must repeal all camping ordinances and rules in the city limits. Recent legal decisions require no contact without offering permanent housing.

5. The City must sanction Camp James Talib-Dean on the Benjamin Franklin Parkway as permanent, legal, valid, and a NO POLICE ZONE.

---

2. See Philadelphia Housing Action's "Our Demands", https://philadelphiahousingaction. info/our-demands/

6. The City must sanction other encampments across the city in spaces that we choose and that will be self-funded and self-governed.

7. The City must immediately stop all Service Days, Encampment Resolutions Homeless Sweeps, or any other activities that harass unhoused people.

The City must support Tiny Houses (not funded by the Low-Income Housing Tax Credit [LIHTC] or any other capitalist scheme) that are self-funded and self-governed by unhoused people. You will not replace any existing or future low-income housing funds to build Tiny Houses.

Demands and Vision:

# The Mission and Vision of the Racial Justice Organizing Committee

### Mission

The Racial Justice Organizing Committee is a group of activists and advocates, working towards the abolition of white supremacy and racism in all the ways it presents in our communities and schools. The goal of racial justice is not to simply reform our current society; the goal is to uproot white supremacy and plant the seeds for liberation and empowerment that will lead to a more just and equitable world. Our Ten Demands for Radical Education Transformation (10 Demands) are foundational towards the vision of racial justice. The 10 Demands, as well as the larger fight for racial justice, will be achieved through purposeful action, building and strengthening relationships between all stakeholders, and continued self-reflection and education.

### What is racial justice?

Racial justice is the abolition of white supremacy and racism in all of the ways it presents in our society—structurally through laws, policies, institutions as well as on a personal and interpersonal level. Racial justice is both theoretical and action oriented. It is an ever-evolving and never-ending process. It requires a historical understanding of how and why we have arrived here in our current state. White supremacy presents itself in myriad ways, through economic oppression due to the racist structure of capitalism, the over-policing of Black communities, under-resourced public schools and neighborhoods, and the lack of safe and equitable housing. Racial justice is inherently intersectional. It requires fighting for and valuing the lives of all Black people which includes the experiences of trans, queer, feminine, and the disabled; regardless of their religion, socioeconomic status, citizenship, age, or educational experience. The goal of racial justice is not to simply reform our current society; the goal is to uproot white supremacy and plant the seeds for a new world.

## What does racial justice look like in schools?

For schools to be sites of racial justice, they need to prioritize, center and protect *all* Black children. In centering the most vulnerable of our Black children, such as Black girls or Black students without housing, it means that the schooling experience of all students regardless of race or identity will improve. A racially just school will allow communities and neighborhoods to determine what is necessary; families should not have to navigate the school choice process. Racially just schools require educators and administrators who are truly accountable to the students and parents they serve, with community control over all aspects of the school. Some specific examples of what racial justice looks in schools are:

- Transformative justice instead of punitive discipline
- Police-free schools—defunding school police to fund other needed resources such as mental health supports
- Equitable funding across the state
- Robust antiracist curriculum that includes African American, ethnic and Indigenous studies for all grade levels with content training for teachers
- Safe and healthy school buildings that function as community centers for everyone
- Ongoing antiracist training for all school and district staff
- Firing of racist teachers and administrators
- Hiring and retaining Black educators—with fully funded pathways for paraprofessionals and high school students to become public school teachers
- Trauma responsive mindset—focus on healing
- Fully funded and staffed special education and ESOL programs at all schools
- Critiquing and eliminating inherently biased practices like standardized testing, uniform policies, software, and grading

## What does racial justice look like in neighborhoods and communities?

The fight for racial justice requires us to move outside of the four walls of classrooms and connect with society at large. The dream of racial justice cannot be realized without fighting for it within and alongside the very communities schools serve. Communities should have the political and economic power to address their unique needs. Schools and communities should be in a reciprocal partnership. Racial justice in communities looks like:

- Functioning and robust community centers
- Community control of land to create green spaces, farms, parks, etc.
- Addressing mental health, violence, poverty, trauma
- Sustainable mutual aid programs
- End to gun violence—programs that address and eliminate the root causes of gun violence
- Living wages for all workers—available jobs and career opportunities in all neighborhoods
- Communities protecting and caring for each other—police and prison abolition
- Government subsidized land/housing for Indigenous people
- Reparations for Black and Indigenous people
- Safe, affordable housing and healthcare for everyone

## Demands and Vision:

# Philly Black Students Alliance (PBSA): Excerpts from their Constitution

**PHILLY BLACK STUDENTS ALLIANCE (PBSA)**
Philadelphia, Pennsylvania
Founded on July 21, 2020

Constitution and Alliance's 10-Point Plan
Drafted August 11, 2020 | Accepted August 19, 2020

Created in July of 2020, the Philly Black Students Alliance (PBSA) was formed to ensure Black students matter in all our schools. We understand that in order for our demands to be accepted, our students, teachers, and alumni across the entire school district must apply pressure. The PBSA seeks to hold individual administrations and the entirety of the district accountable. We believe it is the moral obligation of every individual in the district to be actively engaged in promoting an antiracist learning and living environment and furthermore demand that it be shown through real nonperformative actions. We must see tangible change. *It is time for Black students to be seen, to be heard, to organize.*

Black people, specifically Black students, are not a monolith. However, in our current society we do not have the luxury of not being seen as such. There does not exist one standalone way to experience, express, and embrace the complex identity that is Blackness.

In understanding what it means to be antiracist, you must understand the importance of intersectionality, if in the Alliance's efforts we fail to include brothers and sisters in the LGBTQ+ community, Black women, those of every economic status, and every intersecting identity we have done an inexcusable injustice . . . in neglecting these groups we allow these persons to fall further into isolation. True freedom of the African diaspora can only be achieved when we are all represented. We denounce the differentiation, separation, and crafted selection of "who is Black." There must exist a constant effort to end divisions and promote unity in a world which our presence is so actively attacked. *Together*, inspired by the Pan-African Ideals, we must uplift all Black students: *"It is our duty to fight for our freedom. It is our duty to win. We must love each other and support each other. We have nothing to lose but our chains."* —Assata Shakur

## THE ALLIANCE'S 10-POINT PLAN, PERTAINING TO THE COLLECTIVE DEMANDS OF BLACK STUDENTS
(inspired by the Black Panther Party's Ten-Point Program)

**We want the Freedom and Power to determine the destiny of Black education, understanding our position in a system designed to enforce Black subordination we demand that our voices be heard in all initiatives!**

Black people must be at the forefront of our liberation. We cannot achieve true freedom if we are not leading. Our voices must be featured. We must be in control of our own narrative.

**We want accessibility: Internet access, access to a computer, and to all necessary materials for every Black body in the school district!**

In the digital age, equitable education can only be achieved if all students have equitable access to quality high-speed Internet. Amidst a pandemic, one of the only ways to stay connected is through the Internet, which is no longer a luxury but a necessity. Data shows that Black students are more likely to rely on smartphones to access the Internet. This access is unsuitable for the online classes that every Philly student must attend. We call for public education to only require intellect, and not finances, playing a role in or being a factor in Black students' success.

**We want an education that highlights the splendor of the Black community. We want the uncompromised celebration of Blackness!**

We want an education that unifies Black students and highlights the current and past rich culture that stems from our ancestors and the land of Africa. We want pure expressions of Blackness untainted by the white supremacist agenda—this is the true key to freedom!

We call for the end of every effort that tells students they cannot speak and write in AAVE (African American Vernacular English). We understand English itself is a bastardized language—from the Germanic language family and mixed with Greek, Spanish, and French. The American English spoken form is even more convoluted. We ask why is it okay for white settlers to develop their own vernacular English but African-descended people who have had their languages stolen cannot?

We call for an end of every education system that continues to teach students false accounts of American history inspired by white savior narratives. Understanding this nation was created by the hands of enslaved Black bodies it is crucial that it be taught as such. Subsequently, African American history classes/courses/and all academic endeavors regarding the African diaspora must be taught by those adequately equipped to share this history. *"We believe in an educational system that will give to our people a knowledge of the self. If you do not have knowledge of yourself and your position in the society and in the world, then you will have little chance to know anything else." —Black Panther Party,* The Ten-Point Program

**We want Black educators! We want connections with teachers!**

Education and going to school must not be a burden to Black students. We must be supported by our educators to thrive. Black educators see beyond the opportunity gap that Black students experience and instill confidence necessary for academic achievement. We call for the recruitment and hiring of more Black educators. We demand that Black educators be not only appreciated but furthermore respected by all students, staff, and administrators.

**We want Black student representation in every inter-school governing body, we want an end to all systems that prevent Black representation in student governments and positions of leadership!**

We call for the removal of all barriers such as attendance, GPA, and any other irrelevant qualifications for leadership positions that restrict Black students from being eligible. We demand student government populations include Black students; any governing body that fails to represent all demographics is inherently racist.

**We want an immediate end to all police in schools and an immediate end to all aggressive systems in schools!**

Understanding policing disproportionately affects Black bodies, it serves no place in our schools. We call for the reallocation of police funding into our educational systems. Furthermore, the PBSA stands in full support of the Philadelphia Student Union's "Police Free Schools" initiatives.

**We want the protection of Black women!**

We will not allow misogyny or the patriarchy to erase those who identify as female from the movement, and we will not tolerate the mistreatment of these persons in our schools. Understanding Black women are and always have been essential to organizing, we will uplift all of them in daily practice and through the work we do within PBSA. We call for the end of all systems that oppress our Black sisters: we call for the end of dress codes that serve no other purpose than to perpetuate the adultification and vilification of Black girls which is so deeply rooted in the country's history. Understanding this, and all other oppressive systems deprive Black women of their youth and force white assimilation upon them, we call for the end of any system that favors women of only one economic standing or race. *"Any feminism that privileges those who already have privilege is bound to be irrelevant to poor women, working class women, women of color, trans women, and trans women of color . . . revolutionary hope resides precisely among those women who have been abandoned by history and who are now standing up and making their demands heard."* *--Angela Davis*

**We want the end to oppressive testing systems. We want a complete reevaluation of all testing that does not foster true learning but rather serves as a reinforcement of white supremacy.**

Understanding these testing systems have repeatedly done an injustice to the Black community, we call for assessments in which their outcome is undetermined by one's available economic resources.

**We want an end to colorist and elitist sentiments; any idea that further divides the Black community effectively hinders our movement's success and inevitable freedom! We will not accept nor subscribe to respectability politics!**

We will not allow any teacher or any administration to divide us and use respectability politics or actions of a performative nature as a vehicle to bring about change to education. We will stand together, united and committed to these principles.

### 2020–2021 Leadership

Before the start of the school year, in late August, we officiated the PBSA by taking on leadership roles which are as follow for the 2020–2021 school year:

**Alliance Chairperson(s):** Tatyana Roldan, Brandon Archer, and Sheyla Street

**Secretary:** Makayla Coleman

**Outreach Coordinator(s):** Youma Diabira

**Event Coordinator(s):** Aniyah Harris and Shamiyah Boozer

**Social Media/ Communications Coordinator(s):** Samyah Smalley

**Treasurer:** Rebecca Allen

**Non-Student Representatives (NSRs):** Dr. Ginneh L. Akbar, Hannah Gann, Keziah Ridgeway, Elizabeth Wesley (NSR Treasurer), Mariame Sissoko

Demands and Vision:

# An Open Letter from Concerned Black Workers at the Free Library of Philadelphia[3]

After meeting with several Black employees of the Free Library to share our experiences and concerns, we have determined that racial discrimination and disregard for Black safety, success, prosperity, and life at the Library will no longer be tolerated.

- At the Library, Black staff routinely experience racial discrimination, harassment, microaggressions, and other forms of workplace bias.
- Black staff at the Library are largely relegated to nonprofessional positions, including custodians, municipal guards, and library assistants, and therefore earn $7,533 less than the median salary, while white staff earn $12,012 more than the median salary.
- Black Americans "experience the highest overall mortality rates and the most widespread occurrence of disproportionate deaths" due to COVID-19. Our mortality rate is "2.3 times as high as the rate for whites and Asians, and 2.2 times as high as the Latino rate."
- Armed white vigilante groups patrol areas of Philadelphia where Black staff are asked to return to work.

Black staff at the Free Library of Philadelphia have serious concerns about our health and safety. Our pre-COVID work was on the frontlines, serving Philadelphians in a manner that requires face-to-face activity that makes us most vulnerable to infection. Now is the time for the Free Library to be antiracist. We cannot return to business as usual and must find different and better ways to serve the public while keeping our staff and patrons safe. We are calling for accountability and action regarding the Free Library's plan to protect Black workers as PA moves through the Yellow and Green phases.

We demand the following immediately, before any Black staff are required to report to any Free Library locations.

---

3. Reprinted with permission from the Concerned Black Workers of the Free Library of Philadelphia. Learn more about them at https://www.instagram.com/changetheflp/.

1. A commitment to protecting Black lives on staff.
2. A formal and transparent investigation of Black staff's concerns regarding physically reporting to Free Library locations. Current decisions were made using a misleading survey.
3. A plan, developed with Black staff, to provide Library services that take into account Black people's increased to COVID-19 infection and mortality rates.
4. Support and accommodations for Black staff whose Library work makes them susceptible to racial violence.
5. Provide Black staff the same opportunities to work from home that white staff have.
6. We demand that staff with librarian degrees who work in management, executive, and specialty positions are redeployed to cover the shortages in staff due to COVID-19 and the layoffs of seasonal employees, most of whom are Black.

Now is the time for Library leadership to listen to Black staff, root out institutional racism, and make good on your public statement that #BlackLivesMatter.

Sincerely,
Concerned Black Workers of the Free Library of Philadelphia

# Outreach email and letters to support the campaign to #FreeAntSmith[4]

## [Email Template]

Dear _____,

I am writing to ask for your support to ensure community leader Anthony Smith does not become yet another person removed by the police from his family, friends and community. Standing in solidarity with Ant as a community will be critical to winning his case. See below for how you can take action.

### #FreeAntPHL Call To Action

#### Who is Anthony Smith?

Anthony Smith is a respected educator, a graphic designer, a standout organizer, a powerful leader, and a beloved community member with a passion for making sure everyone around him is protected and thriving.

As a high school social studies teacher in North Philadelphia, he is known for the genuine connections he builds with his students inside and outside the classroom. He is an organizer and volunteer with multiple organizations throughout Philadelphia and is a fixture at 60th and Market each Friday, where he serves free food to the community with Food Not Bombs. His coworkers, students, colleagues, and fellow organizers praise him as an empathetic and reliable peacemaker who always advocates for underrepresented and disenfranchised community members.

---

4. Ed note: We provide this documentation of the call-to-action to honor the local organizing of #FreeAntPHL while simultaneously recognizing its value to serve as a template for inspiring participatory defense campaigns for the freedom of criminalized people. We hope that readers may engage with it in that way: to utilize its framework to kickstart local campaigns for the freedom of criminalized people and political prisoners worldwide.

Anthony has a positive impact in Philadelphia and beyond. To learn more about Ant, see these testimonies celebrating Ant's powerful presence in people's lives.[5]

## What happened?

Anthony was arrested on politically motivated charges as part of a concerted effort to suppress the Black Lives Matter uprisings, and to undermine those with powerful voices calling for justice.

On October 26th, 2020, Anthony was arrested and taken from his home by federal officers based on his alleged involvement in the arson of a police vehicle during a Black Lives Matter protest in May 2020. If convicted, he will face a mandatory minimum of 7 years in prison.

Following his arrest by federal officers, a huge outpouring of community support mobilized to protest the arrest. Anthony received over 70 letters attesting to his selflessness and dedication to serving his community. The school where he works and the organizations where he volunteers his time immediately released statements to express their support[6]. A social media campaign focused on freeing Ant quickly gained national traction.

Anthony was released pretrial and is on a location monitoring program until his court date. As of December 2021, Anthony is still awaiting trial.

## What can you do to support the campaign to Free Ant?
- **Contribute to the costs** necessary for mounting an effective legal campaign to win the case: paypal.me/freeantPHL, CashApp @ freeantPHL or Venmo @FreeAntPHL

  - Our goal is to raise $50,000 to cover the legal and other costs associated with the campaign.

- **Spread the word** about the case with family, friends, colleagues and community members: **community support will make a difference in the outcome of the case.**

---

5. To see the submitted testimonies, visit https://bit.ly/testimoniestofreeant.

6. To see the organizational testimonies, visit https://bit.ly/orgtestimoniestofreeant

- **Follow the campaign** on social media and be prepared to take action closer to the court date:
  - @FreeAntPHL
  - #FreeAntPHL

- **Learn about the broader issues:** This is not just about Ant. It is about standing up and pushing back against aggressive suppression of dissent, and also against the injustices in the prison system that are devastating oppressed communities. Take this moment to learn more about suppressing dissent, and bigger injustices in the system.

# Bibliography

## Liberation Reading List

Extensive reading lists were submitted by the editors and crowdsourced from the contributors of the anthology. They are not exhaustive, but suggestions meant to offer deeper context for Black Philadelphia history, Black radical political education, and insight for personal transformation.

### Black Philadelphia History

Abu-Jamal, Mumia. *We Want Freedom: A Life in the Black Panther Party*. Brooklyn: Common Notions, 2016.

Africa Jr., Mike. *Fifty years on a MOVE*. Self-published, 2021. Available from https://mikeafricajr.com/.

Baker-Rogers, Allener M., and Fasaha Traylor. *They Carried Us: The Social Impact of Philadelphia's Black Women Leaders*. Philadelphia: Arch Street Press, 2020.

Countryman, Matthew. *Up South: Civil Rights and Black Power in Philadelphia*. Philadelphia: University of Pennsylvania Press, 2006.

DuBois, W.E.B. *The Philadelphia Negro: A Social Study*. Centennial ed. Philadelphia: University of Pennsylvania Press, 1999.

Hartman, Saidiya V. *Wayward Lives, Beautiful Experiments: Intimate Histories of Social Upheaval*. New York: W.W. Norton & Company, 2019.

### Personal Transformation

Lorde, Audre. *Sister Outsider: Essays and Speeches*. Trumansburg, NY: Crossing Press, 1984.

Morrison, Toni. *Beloved*. New York: Penguin Books, 2000.

Muller, Lauren, and June Jordan. *June Jordan's Poetry for the People: A Revolutionary Blueprint*. New York: Routledge, 1995.

Shakur, Assata, and Lennox S. Hinds. *Assata: An Autobiography*. Westport, CT: Lawrence Hill & Company, 1987.

Taylor, Sonya Renee. *The Body Is Not an Apology: The Power of Radical*

*Self-Love.* Oakland: Berrett-Koehler Publishers, Inc., 2018.

X, Malcolm, and Alex Haley. *The Autobiography of Malcolm X.* New York: Ballantine Books, 1992.

## Political Education

Ahmad, Muhammad. *We Will Return in the Whirlwind: Black Radical Organizations 1960–1975.* Chicago: Charles H. Kerr. 2008.

brown, adrienne marie. *Emergent Strategy: Shaping Change, Changing Worlds.* Chico: AK Press, 2017.

Davis, Angela Y., and Robin D. G Kelley. *The Meaning of Freedom.* San Francisco: City Lights Books,2012.

Kaba, Mariame. *We Do This 'Til We Free Us: Abolitionist Organizing and Transforming Justice.* Chicago: Haymarket Books. 2021.

Robeson, Paul. *Here I Stand.* Boston: Beacon Press, 1988.

Taylor, Keeanga-Yamahtta. *From #BlackLivesMatter to Black Liberation.* Chicago: Haymarket Books, 2016.

## Uncategorized

Butler, Octavia E. *Parable of the Sower.* New York: Warner Books, 2000.

Redmond, Shana L. *Everything Man: The Form and Function of Paul Robeson.* Durham: Duke University Press, 2020.

Roberts, John W. *ODUNDE Presents From Hucklebuck to Hip-Hop: Social Dance in the African American Community in Philadelphia.* Philadelphia: ODUNDE, Inc., 1995.

Sanchez, Sonia, and Jacqueline Wood. *I'm Black When I'm Singing, I'm Blue When I Ain't and Other Plays.* Durham: Duke University Press, 2010.

Spady, James G., Stefan Dupres, and Charles G. Lee. *Twisted Tales: In the Hip Hop Streets of Philly.* Philadelphia: Black History Museum, UMUM/LOH Publishers, 1995.

Wideman, John Edgar. *Philadelphia Fire: A Novel.* New York: Vintage Books, 1991.

# About the Contributors

**Mike Africa Jr.** is an activist, writer, and the host of the podcast *Ona Move with Mike Africa Jr.* He is the star of the HBO Max documentary *40 Years a Prisoner* (2020), a stage performer, keynote speaker, and a hip-hop artist. Mike was born in a Philadelphia jail following a police raid on his parents' home that led to their arrest and sentence of 100 years in prison. At age six, he witnessed the smoke in the air from a police bomb that was dropped on his family's home, killing his uncle, his cousin, and nine other family members. At age thirteen, he began working to free his parents, and at age forty, after more than twenty-five years of struggle and with the help of his family and attorney Brad Thomson Mike, Mike got his parents out of prison.

**Rasheed Ajamu** is a Black, fat, and queer jawn organizing in digital and communal spaces. He is a self-pronounced Servant Leader to Black Philadelphians, as his mission is to serve as he leads and lead as he serves. He elevates stories and opportunities to aid Black folks, which includes mutual aid, political education, and loads of joy. Sometimes he writes, and sometimes you hear him on *The Gworlz Room* podcast. His mission is to make information accessible to marginalized folks who are most affected by gatekeeping in academia.

**Gabriel Bryant** is an organizer and youth advocate for groups that have included Sankofa Community Empowerment and Philadelphia Community Bail Fund.

**Jasmine L. Combs** is a writer, editor, and teaching artist from Philadelphia. She is the author of two poetry collections: *Universal Themes* (2014) and *This Drowning Was a Baptism* (2019). Her work has been published in literary journals such as *Apiary*, *Vagabond City Lit*, *Vinyl Poetry*, *Painted Bride Quarterly*, and *Prolit*. Jasmine was the 2015 Philly Pigeon Grand Slam Champion and won the 2016 College Union Poetry Slam Invitational. Her work focuses on the intersecting relationships between Blackness, womanhood, mental illness, family, love, and home.

**Jeannine Cook** is a writer, educator, and curator. She is also shopkeeper at Harriett's Bookshop in Philly and Ida's Bookshop in Collingswood, New Jersey.

**Matthew Early** is a father and community advocate currently incarcerated at SCI Coal Township, whose home is the Olney neighborhood of Philadelphia.

**Flare** lives in Philadelphia and organizes with the Black Philly Radical Collective.

**Charlyn Griffith** is an interdisciplinary artist, social scientist, and cultural worker. Charlyn's arts background started in dance and theater and was borne out of the cultural zeitgeist of the 1980s–1990s. They have been shaped by the overlap of their Caribbean upbringing in the US and their English immigrant experiences.

**Corey Hariston** is a Philadelphia-based photographer, widely versatile in the art of photography, but his passion is candid storytelling and environmental portraiture. "The reason why I take pictures of random people on the streets is because I love when a person is living in their natural state, when they're free and in their own little world."

**Jena Harris** is the cofounder of the West Philly Bunny Hop and has worked in food cooperatives in Philadelphia for several years. She is always looking for ways to fuse her food work with the broader community.

**Christian Hayden** is a facilitator, poet, and photographer who lives in Philadelphia, but was born in New York. Christian interns remotely with the Ethical Society of St. Louis, where he gets to put his values of creativity, reflection, and connecting into daily practice. Christian hopes to read, write, and love more as he continues his searching.

**Robert Saleem Holbrook** has a long history of community organizing. He cofounded the Human Rights Coalition and previously served as the Abolitionist Law Center's Director of Community Organizing, a role in which he oversaw the organization's expansion into abolitionist organizing and litigation in the City of Philadelphia. He also led and participated in ALC's advocacy and litigation campaigns against long-term solitary confinement and death by incarceration sentences.

**Nadera Hood** is one of the leading organizers and activists in the #OccupyPHA movement, the occupation of Camp Teddy, and the resulting community land trust to help homeless Philadelphians gain housing through the city's numerous vacancies.

**Dr. Nina Johnson** is an associate professor in the Department of Sociology and Anthropology and the Program in Black Studies at Swarthmore College.

**Sterling Johnson** is a housing lawyer and organizer with Philadelphia Housing Action.

**Stephanie Keene** is a Philadelphia-based writer and creative. She owns Incense, Trap, & Yoga, an apparel line that promotes a culture of justice. Her justice work focuses on decarceration and decriminalization. Stephanie is the program manager for Ethical Global Learning at the Center for Peace and Global Citizenship at Haverford College. A proud graduate of the first HBCU, Lincoln University, she is working for the freedom of all people.

**Nilé Livingston** is a visual artist and the founder of Creative Repute, a graphic design and website development agency. Their work as an artist has been recognized by Rad Girls, The Colored Girls Museum, and Mural Arts Philadelphia. Vernoca Michael, the recently retired executive director of the West Philly Cultural Alliance, awarded Livingston their first official residency at the Paul Robeson House. What might be considered a typical forward motion in an artist's career—a residency—was an unexpected and unsolicited gift that placed them in responsible dialogue with historical Black cultural workers.

**Jared Michael Lowe** is a writer who covers arts, fashion, beauty, sexuality, gender, race, and popular culture. His work has appeared in *NBC News*, *Cosmopolitan*, *Teen Vogue*, *HuffPost*, and *EBONY*. In addition, he's a contributing editor for *Root Quarterly*, a Philadelphia-based print literary journal of art and ideas.

**Koren Martin** is a Philadelphia-based photographer originally from Atlantic City, New Jersey. Her work is a mixture of candid portraiture and immersive documentary photography. She has passion for highlighting the beauty and strength of the African diaspora. Her current photo series, "Birthing the Resistance," is a celebration of Black mothers who are involved in activism. She received honorable mention in *MFON: Women Photographers of the African Diaspora*, a biannual journal committed to establishing and representing a collective voice of women photographers of African descent. Her work has been exhibited in Photoville 2018, Your Art Gallery, The Black Joy Archive (2020), and the PPAC-Everyone of Us Campaign (2020).

**DuiJi Mshinda** is a veteran of the West Philadelphia poetry scene. He organized and hosted events for a decade before pivoting into a consistent DJ ministry. His poetry discusses poverty, discrimination, mental health stigma, incarceration, and family life.

**Abdul-Aliy Abdullah Muhammad** is a Philadelphia-born writer and organizer. They often write about Blackness, bodily autonomy, and medical surveillance.

**YahNé Ndgo** is a member of Black Lives Matter Philly, the outreach coordinator and a member of the Coordinating Committee for the Black Alliance for Peace, and works in partnership with other organizers toward Black and Indigenous solidarity.

**Malkia Okech** is a Philadelphia-based researcher, cultural producer, and community archaeologist. She is interested in the cross sections of multimodal archaeology, art, technology, cultural heritage, anticapitalism, and liberation. Malkia graduated from the University of Pennsylvania in 2019 with degrees in Near Eastern Language and Civilization and Digital Humanities. She is the associate producer for Black Spatial Relics, an artist residency and annual convening exploring slavery, justice, and freedom. She is an Activist-Curator Fellow for the Free Library and PASCAL consortium, where she is doing abolitionist research and community archive building. She is the founder and curator of Memory Studio, an interdisciplinary makerspace reckoning with decolonial knowledge accumulation, production, and speculation.

She does local movement work with autonomous abolitionist collectives, and her praxis is formed by the past, present, and future continuum of freedom-dreaming.

**Meg Onli** is an art curator and writer. She is currently the Andrea B. Laporte Associate Curator at the Institute of Contemporary Art in Philadelphia. Her curatorial work primarily revolves around the Black experience, language, and constructions of power and space.

**Ewuare X. Osayande** is a poet, educator, and publisher. He is founder of Freedom Seed Press and the author of several books of poetry, including: *Whose America?* and *Black Phoenix Uprising*. He is also director of ORIJIN, which provides racial-justice consultation for organizations and educational institutions.

**Cassie Owens** is a writer and reporter, currently covering sociocultural dynamics—as well as how Philadelphians contend with them these days—at *The Philadelphia Inquirer*.

**Joe Piette** is a Philadelphia-based writer and photographer covering local social, political, and civil actions.

**Jaz Riley** is a PhD candidate at Yale University and prior to this, was military personnel. Jaz has a master's degree in English and a MPhils in African American Studies and American Studies. Jaz serves as strategist and copywriter for Creative Repute. In their spare time, Jaz enjoys reading about both lighthearted topics and important Black and Brown politics. Their work is informed by their everyday life as a Southern-raised, well-traveled, educated Black person.

**Tafari Robertson** is a multidisciplinary artist from Austin, Texas, currently living in West Philadelphia with his cat, Marcia. His practice involves moving fluidly between creative projects and mediums, exploring new ways to preserve Black cultural spaces and experiences. He enjoys Caribbean food, kite-flying, and fresh fruit.

**Sheyla Street** is a student, activist, and varsity athlete. From leading her school's voter registration team to helping found the Philly Black Students Alliance to pushing her school to implement Black students' demands, Sheyla works to mobilize her peers to move forward an agenda of impact and change. An advocate of Philly Youth Vote, Sheyla has been testifying at school board meetings since 2019 to get a voter education and registration policy implemented. As both President of Central's National Honor Society and member of the Black Student Council, Sheyla helps to tutor and mentor students at local elementary and middle schools to increase Black and Brown student recruitment. Whether it is mental health, student empowerment, or moving forward the demands of Black students from across the city, Sheyla organizes as PBSA's chairperson. Sheyla is also a PIAA state-qualified track athlete and is 4x All-Public in Philadelphia.

**Krystal Strong** is an organizer and a scholar from Philadelphia whose political work, research, and teaching focus on student and community activism, preserving Black Philadelphia, and the role of education as a site of struggle in Africa and the diaspora. Krystal is a core organizer with Black Lives Matter Philly, Black Philly Radical Collective, and is an assistant professor at the University of Pennsylvania's Graduate School of Education.

**Yolanda Wisher** is the author of *Monk Eats an Afro* and served as the third Poet Laureate of Philadelphia in 2016 and 2017. She performs a unique blend of poetry and song with her band The Afroeaters and works as the Curator of Spoken Word at Philadelphia Contemporary.

# About the Editors

**Fajr Muhammad** is a writer and editor from Philadelphia, Pennsylvania. She earned her MFA in Fiction from Columbia University and B.A. in English with a minor in Women's Studies from Kutztown University. Her writing has been featured in the *Columbia Journal Online* and *The Hennepin Review* and she was recently named 2021 runner-up for the Marianne Russo novel-in-progress award with the Key West Literary Seminar. Her work has received fellowships from the *Tin House* Summer Writers' Workshop, the Rhode Island Writers Colony and the Jack Jones Literary Arts Retreat. She sits on the Blue Stoop advisory board, a nonprofit dedicated to Philadelphia writers.

**Christopher R. Rogers** is an educator and cultural worker from Chester, Pennsylvania. He serves as Public Programs Director for the Paul Robeson House & Museum , where he has volunteered since 2015. Additionally, he is currently a doctoral student within the University of Pennsylvania Graduate School of Education where he studies neighborhood storytelling practices in West Philadelphia. He serves on the National Steering Committee for Black Lives Matter at School, supporting movements for racial justice in K-16 education.

**The West Philadelphia Cultural Alliance** is the certified non-profit which operates the Paul Robeson House & Museum, located at 4951 Walnut St. The mission of The West Philadelphia Cultural Alliance (WPCA) / Paul Robeson House & Museum (PRHM) is to cultivate interest and support for the arts in West Philadelphia; to increase the visibility of West Philadelphia's rich cultural resources; and to promote positive social change in our community through the arts. The WPCA was founded in 1984 by Frances P. Aulston and extends the contributions of Paul Robeson, who combined artistic excellence with profound political and social activism. The West Philadelphia Cultural Alliance implement programs that blend these shared visions and increase awareness of Robeson's trailblazing life, legacy, and philosophy for our local and global communities. The Paul Robeson House & Museum is listed on the U.S. National Register of Historic Places.

## About Common Notions

Common Notions is a publishing house and programming platform that advances new formulations of liberation and living autonomy. Our books provide timely reflections, clear critiques, and inspiring strategies that amplify movements for social justice.

By any media necessary, we seek to nourish the imagination and generalize common notions about the creation of other worlds beyond state and capital. Our publications trace a constellation of critical and visionary meditations on the organization of freedom. Inspired by various traditions of autonomism and liberation—in the United States and internationally, historically and emerging from contemporary movements—our publications provide resources for a collective reading of struggles past, present, and to come.

Common Notions regularly collaborates with editorial houses, political collectives, militant authors, and visionary designers around the world. Our political and aesthetic interventions are dreamt and realized in collaboration with Antumbra Designs.

commonnotions.org / info@commonnotions.org

## Become a Monthly Sustainer

These are decisive times, ripe with challenges and possibility, heartache and beautiful inspiration. More than ever, we are in need of timely reflections, clear critiques, and inspiring strategies that can help movements for social justice grow and transform society. Help us amplify those necessary words, deeds, and dreams that our liberation movements and our worlds so need.

Movements are sustained by people like you, whose fugitive words, deeds, and dreams bend against the world of domination and exploitation.

For collective imagination, dedicated practices of love and study, and organized acts of freedom.

By any media necessary. With your love and support.
Monthly sustainers start at $12 and $25.
Join us at commonnotions.org/sustain.

# More From Common Notions

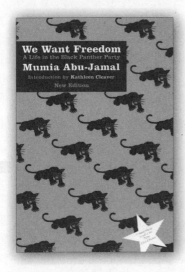

*We Want Freedom: A Life in the Black Panther Party*
New Edition

Mumia Abu-Jamal
Introduction by Kathleen Cleaver

978-1-942173-04-5
$20
336 pages

Mumia Abu-Jamal, America's most famous political prisoner, is internationally known for his radio broadcasts and books emerging "Live from Death Row." In his youth Mumia Abu-Jamal helped found the Philadelphia branch of the Black Panther Party, wrote for the national newspaper, and began his life-long work of exposing the violence of the state as it manifests in entrenched poverty, endemic racism, and unending police brutality. In *We Want Freedom*, Mumia combines his memories of day-to-day life in the Party with analysis of the history of Black liberation struggles. The result is a vivid and compelling picture of the Black Panther Party and its legacy.

# More From Common Notions

*Abolishing Carceral Society*
Abolition Collective

978-1-942173-08-3
$20.00
256 pages
20 Illustrations

In the first of a series of publications, the Abolition Collective renews and boldly extends the tradition of "abolition-democracy" espoused by figures like W.E.B. Du Bois, Angela Davis, and Joel Olson. Through study and publishing, the Abolition Collective supports radical scholarly and activist research, recognizing that the most transformative scholarship is happening both in the movements themselves and in the communities with whom they organize.

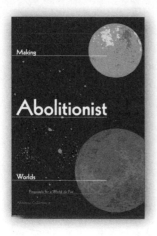

*Making Abolitionist Worlds*
Abolition Collective

978-1-942173-17-5
$20.00
272 pages

*Making Abolitionist World*s gathers key insights and interventions from today's international abolitionist movement to pose the question: what does an abolitionist world look like? The Abolition Collective investigates the core challenges to social justice and the liberatory potential of social movements today from a range of personal, political, and analytical points of view, underscoring the urgency of an abolitionist politics that places prisons at the center of its critique and actions.